Pattern #
Simplicity 6790

5185 Suit
6624 Sweater
or Top

7 Zipper
Scissors
Pins

# How to Sew Fashion Knits

Published by THE SINGER COMPANY

Dear Reader:

How to Sew Fashion Knits is your key to a new world of sewing pleasure.

As the recommended textbook for SINGER courses in sewing knits, it contains a great deal of helpful reference material relating to projects made in class. In addition, it covers a wide range of other types of knit sewing projects. Thus, you will find it a valuable reference long after you complete your SINGER course.

Moreover, How to Sew Fashion Knits is much more than merely a book of instructions. It tells you the "why" as well as the "how." Once armed with this understanding, you will be able to approach any pattern — even those not designed for knits — with confidence.

Best of all, your understanding of construction principles will free you to sew creatively. You will be able to adapt patterns as you like, to make exciting knit fashions that are yours alone.

Franklin A. Kolyer
Director of Education
THE SINGER COMPANY

# TABLE OF CONTENTS

# FABRIC FACTS

Fashioning knit fabric into your own personalized wardrobe is a fascinating new way to sew. Knits have been on the market for the home sewer for quite a few years now, and the selection gets bigger all the time. In fact, you can find the same yardage in fabric stores that you see made up in the ready-to-wear section of department stores. There are many stores all over the country now that specialize in knit fabric and the trims and elastic needed to go with it. It's available – so let's learn to use it.

## TYPES OF KNIT FABRICS

Some of the different types of knit fabrics are described below. You will soon become familiar with them and get to know their different characteristics.

It is important that you select the right type of knit fabric for the garment that you are making. Some knits can be used for almost anything, while others are more limited in their application.

**SINGLE KNITS** are lightweight fabrics made from many different fibers. They are made on machines with only one set of needles and have a definite right and wrong side. Many times you will find these knits in a tube form. Single knits do not keep their shape as well as doubleknits, so they are not suitable for pants and straight skirts.

Pattern Choice: This type of knit adapts well to the skinny look and is used for many sport tops. Look for patterns with soft details such as gathers, eased fullness, and draping. Collars, cuffs, and other details will have to be interfaced to add body.

Types of Garments: Sporty, casual, or dressy as the fabric indicates. Used mainly for tops, gathered skirts, and dresses. Also men's shirts and children's wear.

**DOUBLEKNITS** are firm, costume-weight knits that are a delight to use. They are made on machines that have two beds of needles that produce a fabric that is really two single layers knitted together. The fabric will appear to be the same on both sides unless a texture or pattern is knitted into it. Doubleknits hold their shape well.

Pattern Choice: Look for patterns with simple style lines because this type of knit is thick and does not adapt well to gathered styles. Seam shaping, darts, eased fullness, and soft pleats are suitable. Beautiful pocket, collar, and banding details can be achieved. Topstitching is also very attractive.

Types of Garments: Dresses, suits, pants, skirts, shirts, vests, lightweight coats, children's and menswear.

## WARP KNITS

are made on very intricate knitting machines that produce fabrics with vertical rows of loops on the right side and horizontal rows of loops on the wrong side. These knits are generally firmer than doubleknits and less apt to snag. Many of the new menswear fabrics are warp knits.

Raschel knits are a type of warp knit. They are made on special knitting machines that produce fabrics with lacy open-work designs.

Pattern Choice: Firm warp knits adapt well to almost any pattern. The raschel knits generally have much surface detail, so patterns should be selected that have simple lines.

Types of Garments: Dresses, tops, pants, vests, and skirts.

## SWEATER KNITS

look and act like hand knits. They stretch freely in both directions, shape to the body, and many times have a loose, lofty look. You will find these knits with a ribbed, textured, or flat surface.

Sweater bodies are tubes of sweater knit that have a ribbed bottom. They come in various widths and lengths, so make sure that you buy enough to make a complete sweater. They are treated in the manufacturing process so that they will not ravel when cut. Matching strips of ribbing are generally available to be used for neckline trims.

Pattern Choice: Use special knit patterns or patterns that are marked "for knits only". Sweater knits can be sewn with little or no ease in the pattern. Use straight styles with no darts.

Types of Garments: Dresses, tops, vests, and pants.

**LINGERIE KNITS**
**(tricot)**

are a type of warp knit. They are made from nylon yarns in sheer, medium, and heavy weights. The greatest stretch is across the width of the fabric, and they are sometimes as wide as 108 inches.

Pattern Choice: Look for lingerie patterns from the regular pattern catalogues or use some of the special knit lingerie patterns that are available.

Types of Garments: Slips, panties, sleepwear, and scarfs.

**SPANDEX**

or power net is a knit fabric with great strength and stretch. It is used for undergarments, in swim and ski wear, and also in some delicate laces. It is stronger and more durable than rubber, and it has two-way stretch.

Pattern Choice: Look for special knit patterns designed for undergarments and swimwear.

Types of Garments: Bras, girdles, swimsuits and ski pants.

**RIBBING**

is a special knit fabric that is used to trim neck and arm openings on knit tops and dresses. It is made to have lots of stretch but will bounce back to its original size. It comes by the yard and is then cut into narrow strips. Do not pre-shrink ribbing.

## KNIT FIBERS

Knit yardage is made from many different kinds of fibers. You will find delicate lace, heavy-duty nylon suitable for sports or swimwear, glitter and metallic knits for evening wear, single and double-knits to be fashioned into all kinds of garments, and sweater knits for making sweaters and dresses. It is important, though, that you know the type of knit you are working with so that you will know how to clean it properly and the correct temperature setting to use on your iron. Most knits are washable, which is one reason that they are so popular. But some, such as wool and some acetates, must be dry-cleaned. Check the bolt ends for fiber content when you are buying knits to determine the type of care required.

You are all familiar with the popular cotton-knit top that you buy one or two sizes too large because it will shrink in the washing process. This is a characteristic of most knits and one that must be understood if you are to have good results with your sewing. Wouldn't it be nice to shrink the fabric before you make your garment? Then you would not have to worry about the fit after one or two washings or cleanings. This really is not much of a problem if you learn to shrink your fabric before you cut it. This is where knowledge of fiber content is so important. Remember that I said most knits are washable, but some are not. You must know which are and which are not so that you can care for each fabric in the proper way.

The rule to remember is: use the same method to shrink the fabric as you will use when cleaning the garment.

Shrink all cottons, polyesters, wools, acrylics, nylons, acetates, triacetates, and swim fabrics. Do not shrink ribbings or alpaca knit. Remember to allow extra yardage for shrinkage when you buy your fabric. For each yard of cotton needed, buy an extra 4 or 5 inches. Most other fabrics shrink very little, but even a little shrinkage is sometimes enough to make a great difference in the fit, so be sure to allow 2 or 3 extra inches per yard.

The table on the following pages will tell you how to prepare and care for all of the most popular fabrics on the market today.

If, by chance, you have some fabric and are uncertain of its fiber content, you can identify it by a simple test. Touch a burning match to a small scrap of the fabric, and notice how it burns.

<u>Wool</u> will burn slowly and leave a soft, black ash. Also it will smell like hair burning.

<u>Polyester</u> will burn slowly and melt. It will leave a hard, black, round ash.

<u>Nylon</u> will melt very slowly and leave a hard, grey ash.

<u>Acrylic</u> will burn and melt, leaving a hard black ash. Acrylic also turns a darker shade when a steam iron is placed on it.

**COTTON KNIT** is an easy-care and comfortable fabric. It is cool to wear because the fibers absorb body moisture, making it a good choice for summer wear. It is ideal for babies for the same reason and also because it is non-allergenic. Cotton can be machine-washed and dried using a warm or hot temperature.

Cotton comes in single, double, and other types of knits with either a flat or textured surface. Some single-knit cottons tend to roll at the edges after being shrunk. This can be controlled by spraying with fabric finish and then pressing lightly.

Most cottons are knit in a tube or are sewn into a tube after knitting. Cut the tube after the fabric has been shrunk.

When cottons are processed in the mill, they are pressed with a lot of heat and pressure, so permanent creases are found on both sides of the fabric. Avoid these creases when cutting out your fabric.

Cotton does not adapt well to adults' dresses or pants because it will bag in the seat and knee areas. It is acceptable for children's dresses and pants.

**COTTON VELOUR** is a luxurious but machine-washable fabric. Velour has a nap just like velvet, so you must remember to place your pattern pieces on the fabric so that they all face in the same direction.

Velour is beautiful for tops and robes. You will also see it used for making pants and dresses. Since it is made from cotton yarn, it will tend to bag in the seat and knee areas.

**COTTON TERRY** is a stretch fabric with a looped surface. It also has a nap, so care must be taken when placing your pattern on the fabric. Stretch terry makes beautiful baby clothes and knit tops for the whole family.

**WOOL** is one of the most popular knit fabrics because it is easy to work with and warm to wear. Wool is used in single-knit jerseys, sweater knits, and the beautiful doubleknits. You will find this fabric used in practically every type of garment you can imagine. It keeps its shape beautifully and will not sag or bag.

Wool should be dry-cleaned for best results. It should also be shrunk before being cut. The easiest way for the home sewer to do this is to put the dry wool yardage into the home dryer with some other damp clothes. Turn the dryer on and leave the wool in for about 15 minutes. The moisture from the damp clothes and the heat of the dryer will remove any shrinkage. Do not use damp clothes that will put lint on the wool yardage.

Press wool on the wrong side with lots of steam in the seam areas. A pressing cloth is a must with wool.

**RAYON** is a man-made fiber that is used for garments that do not get hard daily wear. Best results are obtained from dry cleaning.

TRADEMARKS: Zantrel   Softglo

**ACETATE** is a cellulose fiber similar to rayon. It comes in a wide range of colors and has a luxurious feel. Most acetate knits should be dry-cleaned.

Occasionally a fabric will be marked washable but care must be used to avoid setting in wrinkles. Use mild, lukewarm suds, gently squeeze them through the fabric, and rinse in lukewarm water. Shake the garment out and let it drip-dry. Press the garment while still damp, on the wrong side, with the iron on the lowest setting.

Perfumes and fingernail-polish remover will adversely affect acetate.

**TRIACETATE** is another cellulose fiber used in many knits. It is shrink- and wrinkle-resistant. It is easily washed and resists fading. Triacetate is permanently pleated quite often for skirts and hostess pants.

It is best to hand-launder pleated garments. Most other triacetates can be machine-washed and dried. A high temperature can be used on the iron.

TRADEMARKS:   Arnel

**NYLON** is a strong, elastic, man-made fiber. It is very abrasion-resistant and easy to wash and dry, so it is ideal for children's and sports clothes. It can be of a very heavy quality, as in swim fabric and Helenca yarn, or very lightweight, as in lingerie fabrics and Ban-Lon yarn.

Wash delicate nylon garments by hand in warm water. Other garments can be washed and dried in the machine. Add a fabric softener in the final rinse, and remove the garment as soon as the dryer stops. Press with a warm iron.

Separate colors when washing nylon because white nylon will pick up any color in the wash water.

TRADEMARKS: Caprolan Enkalure
Antrol Ban-Lon
Helenca

**ACRYLIC** is another man-made fiber that can be knit into a variety of textures and weights. It is used for pants, tops, dresses, suits, and sweaters.

Wash delicate acrylic garments by hand in warm water. Rinse thoroughly and use a fabric softener in the final rinse. Other garments can be machine-washed and dried. Use a low temperature setting in the dryer and remove the garments as soon as the tumbling stops. It is a good idea to turn all acrylic garments inside out before washing. This helps prevent fuzz balls from forming on the outer surface.

TRADEMARKS: Creslan Orlon Acrilan

**POLYESTER** is the miracle fabric of our day. It is wrinkle-resistant, easy to wash and dry, and takes dye beautifully. The perfect traveler's fabric, it can be used for practically any garment you can think of.

Again, wash delicate garments by hand, adding fabric softener in the final rinse. Other garments can be machine-washed and dried. Always use a warm iron to press, and avoid placing the iron on the right side of the fabric without a press cloth.

Grease stains can usually be removed from polyester if you will rub liquid detergent into the stain before washing.

TRADEMARKS: Encron Dacron Kodel
Fortrel Trevira

**POLYESTER-COTTON BLEND** is a good fabric for sportswear. It washes and dries easily and is wrinkle-resistant. Take care with oil-based stains. This fabric has better shape retention than 100% cotton.

**POLYESTER-WOOL BLEND** is a relatively new fabric. It is usually composed of 70% polyester and 30% wool. It has the look and feel of wool but can be machine-washed.

Wash this fabric in warm water and it can be safely dried at a low temperature. Remove it from the dryer immediately after the tumbling action has stopped.

**FIBERFILL** is a soft, fluffy material made from polyester fibers. It is used in bra cups, and any other place where a lightweight, washable padding is needed.

**SPANDEX** can be hand- or machine-washed in lukewarm water. Use an oxygen or sodium perborate bleach instead of a chlorine bleach. It can be machine-dried at a low temperature, but wears better if it is drip-dried.

TRADEMARKS: Lycra Elura

**METALLIC** fabrics are used for dressy evening wear. They are either a plastic-coated metal or a metal-coated plastic. For best results, follow the bolt-end instructions for cleaning care.

**ALPACA** is a sweater knit that you buy by the yard. It is used for sweaters and two-piece dresses. Pure alpaca is imported from Peru. Sometimes an alpaca blend is available that looks like the pure alpaca but is actually a blend of alpaca and wool.

Alpaca should be dry-cleaned for best results. It is not necessary to pre-shrink alpaca but it is a good idea to place the fabric on a flat surface overnight to allow the fabric to relax before you cut it.

# PATTERN FACTS

There are many kinds of patterns available now that are designed just for knit fabrics. These can usually be found in fabric stores that specialize in knits. Now that the large pattern companies have caught on to the knit craze, they are designing some of their patterns especially for knits. As a result, there is a great selection of patterns to choose from, and you will soon find which ones work best for you. The purpose of this book is not to tell you which pattern to buy, but to teach you to take a basic pattern that fits you, and change it into any style that you want. Remember, you are learning techniques that can be used with any pattern, which is what makes sewing with knits so much fun. You begin to be creative. Change your top or dress to make it really yours, and do not be afraid of making mistakes. Mistakes often turn into something quite beautiful because you learn theories and techniques that can rescue what looks like the worst disaster.

## CONVENTIONAL PATTERNS

"Conventional" is the word that I will use to refer to patterns that you can buy from the catalogues displayed in fabric stores. These are the familiar patterns that you have used for years.

As you look through these pattern catalogues you will notice that there are basically three types of patterns: a regular conventional pattern, a recommended-for-knits pattern, and a knits-only pattern. You should understand the differences between these three types of patterns so that you can use them properly.

The Regular Conventional Pattern. These patterns have been designed for use with woven fabric and have a certain amount of ease designed into them. Since woven fabric has no "give," the pattern has to provide the room that you need for movement. Knit fabrics have give, so this extra room, or ease, is not needed. Consequently, you will find that regular conventional patterns will produce a garment that is too large when made from a knit fabric. This problem can be solved by taking larger seam allowances or, sometimes, choosing a pattern one size smaller than your body measurements indicate.

The Recommended-For-Knits Pattern. Patterns that are recommended for knits are labeled this way because of the style, not because they have any less ease than regular patterns. Knits adapt well to patterns that have simple lines and uncomplicated detail. Conventional patterns that fit these requirements are marked "recommended for knits" in order to help you select an appropriate style for your knit fabric. Because these patterns are basically regular conventional patterns, you will run into the sizing problem described above. Take larger seam allowances or choose a smaller size pattern.

The For-Knits-Only Pattern. These patterns are designed to be used with stretchy knit fabrics. They will be much too small if they are made in a woven fabric, which does not give as a knit does. The extra room that you need for movement is provided by the knit fabric. Select these patterns according to your body measurements.

## SPECIAL KNIT PATTERNS

There are some special knit patterns available now, which are simple, basic patterns that have more than one size in the same envelope. This feature makes them very useful because you can use them for more than one person. Also, you may need to use a smaller size than normal when you work with a very stretchy knit fabric.

Special knit patterns have very little detail printed on them. You should look them over carefully before you use them in order to see the seam width that has been allowed and various other things. Many of these patterns allow only a ¼-inch seam allowance, so keep that in mind when you are making the garment.

Special knit patterns are master patterns, and it is recommended that you do not cut them. Trace the pattern onto a large piece of pattern paper so that you can preserve the master pattern and use the other sizes.

## CHOOSING THE PROPER SIZE

The preceding section has covered the differences between the various patterns that are available for your use. The differences are mainly in the amount of ease allowed. This problem is not confined to conventional patterns – it is also found in the special knit patterns. Each pattern company has its own idea of the proper amount of ease to allow, so the amount will vary from one company to another. The only solution to this problem is to decide on the amount of ease you like in your clothes, and then measure the paper pattern to see if that amount is provided.

Generally, 1 to 2 inches of ease around the bust or chest is adequate in a knit fabric. Occasionally, you might want to allow 3 inches for a very loose, casual fit. There should also be at least 1 inch of ease around arms and legs. If you are in doubt about the fit, make an experimental model or measure a knit garment that you already have to see how much ease has been allowed.

A word of caution – different types of knits stretch different amounts. Some are very stretchy and some have hardly any stretch at all. This will influence the size selection also. The figures given above are for the average single-knit and doubleknit fabric. If you select a very stretchy type of knit, you may find a size smaller than you normally use will give you a better-fitting garment.

The special knit patterns come with more than one size in the envelope, so just measure the bust or chest portion of the various sizes until you find one that gives you the desired ease. Remember not to include seam allowances in this measurement. When you find the proper size, do not be surprised if it is not what you think you should wear. Trust your measurements and go ahead. If you are still in doubt – cut a bit larger. You can always take in seams, but it is difficult to add on after the fabric has been cut.

## BASIC PATTERN ALTERATIONS

Now that you have decided on the proper pattern size, you should check a few other body and pattern measurements to see whether any alterations are needed. These are simple to do and will save you lots of problems as you fit the garment.

This section will cover alterations for knit tops and dresses. Altering pants and skirt patterns will be covered later.

Shoulder Width. The width of the shoulder seam on the paper pattern should be equal to your measured shoulder width. Take your measurement, compare it to the pattern's measurement, and adjust the pattern, if necessary.

Measure the distance from the base of your neck out to the bone at the edge of your shoulder. Record this measurement on your pattern.

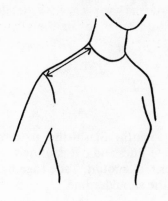

Measure the shoulder seam on the pattern. Do not include the seam allowances in this measurement. — *Runs between 4½ & 5"*

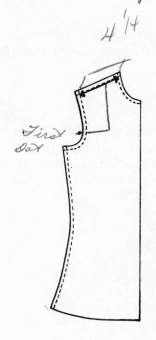

To Add Width: Slash the pattern along the dotted lines. Do not cut the pattern apart at the arm edge. Spread the two pieces apart until you have added the required width. Fill in the gap with a piece of pattern paper, and tape it in place. Re-draw the shoulder line so that it is straight.

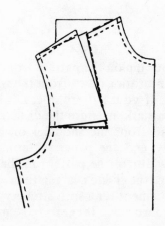

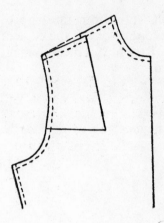

To Subtract Width: Slash the pattern along the same lines and overlap the two pieces the desired amount. Tape together and re-draw the shoulder line.

Hip Width. Check the width of your pattern in the hip area to see whether it is large enough. The pattern should be 1 to 2 inches larger than your hip measurement.

Tie a string around your waist. Measure the fullest part of your hip. Note how far down from the waistline this measurement is taken. Record these two measurements on your pattern.

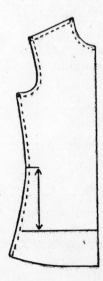

Locate your hip on the pattern front and back by measuring down from the waistline mark. If your pattern does not have a waistline mark, measure the distance to the hipline from the shoulder on both your body and the paper pattern. The finished width of the pattern in the hip area should be 1 inch larger than your hip measurement for a soft, stretchy knit and 2 inches larger for most doubleknits.

**To Add Width:** Make a vertical slash from the bottom edge of the pattern up into the waistline area. Spread the pattern apart the desired amount and then tape in a piece of pattern paper to fill the gap.

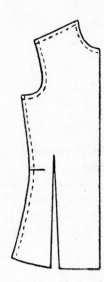

**To Subtract Width:** Trim the side seams the desired amount.

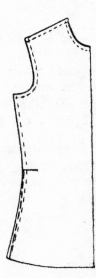

<u>Sleeve Length</u>. Check the length of your sleeve pattern and adjust it before pinning it to the fabric. Allow an extra 1¼ inches for the hem on all lengths. Do not allow for a hem if you are going to sew a strip of ribbing onto the sleeve edge.

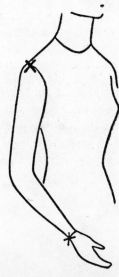

Measure the length of a long sleeve from the point of your shoulder, down around your slightly bent elbow, to the wrist-bone. Record this length and adjust the pattern, if necessary.

Measure the length of a long raglan sleeve by starting the measurement at the base of the neck, over the shoulder point, around the slightly bent elbow, down to the wristbone. Record this measurement and adjust the pattern if necessary.

To Add Length: Cut the pattern apart and spread it the needed amount. Tape it together with an extra piece of paper.

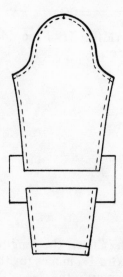

To Subtract Length: Make a fold across the width of the pattern. The width of the fold should be ½ the amount that is to be removed.

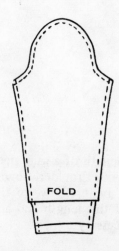

Sleeve Width. The sleeve should be 1 to 2 inches wider than your arm measurements at all points. Allow 2 inches if you have a full arm or are using a firm knit.

Measure your upper arm, forearm, and wrist. Check these measurements against the paper pattern and alter if necessary.

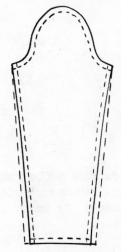

To Add Width: Add an equal amount to both seam allowances.

*Lenght should measure the length of set in sleeve.*

If you need fullness in the extreme upper-arm area also, it would be best to slash the pattern from the bottom, up to but not through the top edge. Spread the pattern apart the desired amount, and tape in an extra piece of paper to fill the gap.

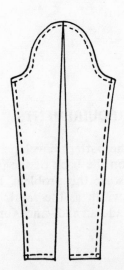

To Subtract Width:  Taper both edges of
the sleeve the desired amount.

Sleeve Cap. On the regular conventional and recommended-for-knits patterns, you will find too much ease allowed in the sleeve cap. This should be altered before you sew the sleeve into the arm opening.

The sleeve pattern that is used with a knit fabric should measure only 1 inch larger than the arm opening. You will find it difficult to get a smooth sleeve cap if you have to work with more than 1 inch of ease. The stretch of the knit fabric will provide the needed ease.

The excess ease can be removed by trimming the curve on each side of the sleeve cap. Remove the same amount from each side.

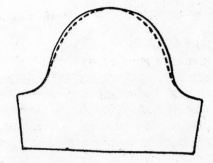

## YARDAGE REQUIREMENTS

Check the pattern envelope for yardage requirements. All conventional patterns will include this information on the back of the pattern envelope, but you will not always find it on the special knit patterns. To solve this problem, lay out the pattern pieces on some newspapers that have been folded to the same width as the fabric that you are going to purchase. Measure the length required, and remember to add an allowance for shrinkage.

Generally, if you buy a sleeve and a body length plus extra for shrinkage, you will have plenty of fabric. Some knit fabrics are wide enough to accomodate the body and sleeve pattern pieces side by side. Children's patterns can usually be cut this way, and it saves on fabric.

Until you get more familiar with yardage requirements for various garments for you and your family, it is a good idea to carry your patterns to the store with you. Most stores will let you take a minute to place the pattern pieces on the fabric so that you can buy just the right amount.

## THE EXPANDED PATTERN

An expanded pattern is very handy to work with when you are making a top or dress from striped fabric. The stripes are much easier to match if you work with a complete pattern piece and pin it to a single layer of fabric. You may wonder why anyone would want to cut only a single layer at a time. Let's discuss striped knits for a bit, and then you will understand why I suggest working with an expanded pattern and a single layer of fabric.

Many striped knit fabrics are made on circular knitting machines. This produces a stripe that spirals around the piece of fabric. It is practically impossible to place two layers of this type of fabric on top of each other and have the stripes match for cutting. It can be done by pushing and patting the stripes into place and then pinning them so that they stay, but this is very time-consuming and not always accurate. It is much easier to work with a single layer of fabric and an expanded pattern. By using the expanded pattern, you can see where the stripes are on both sides of the pattern piece, and it is easy to make sure that they run straight across the width of the pattern.

Some conventional patterns use the expanded pattern in their knits-only series. Most of the special knit patterns use only the half-pattern, so you should learn to make an expanded pattern to be used with striped fabrics.

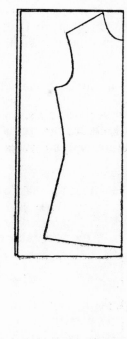

Take a large piece of pattern paper that is the same length as your paper pattern and twice its width. Fold the pattern paper in half lengthwise, and place it on top of the pattern piece. The folded edge should be along the center-front or center-back line. Trace the pattern, marking all notches, circles, and any other pattern markings. Label the new pattern with size, pattern number, and pattern piece.

Cut around the traced pattern while the paper is still folded. You now have an expanded pattern ready to use with your striped fabric.

Follow this procedure for both back and front pattern pieces. If the pattern that you are working with has a center-back seam allowance, you should trim it off or fold it out of the way so that the fold of the pattern paper can run along the center back of the pattern. If you are planning a zipper opening in the garment, you can put it in a slash instead of a seam.

## PATTERN LAYOUT

The pattern layouts for striped and solid-color knits will be different. There are a few things that apply to both types of knits when cutting, so let's discuss these first.

1. Knits should be treated as napped fabrics; that is, the tops of all the pattern pieces should be placed on the fabric so that they face only one end of the fabric. The reason is that knits are made by rows of loops that are interconnected, and the rounded tops of the loops reflect the light differently from the open bottoms. Therefore, knits should be cut so that the tops of the loops run in the same direction, thus preventing color changes from appearing at seamlines.

2. Knits should be cut with the greatest amount of stretch going around the body. The greatest stretch is generally across the width of the fabric.

3. Solid-color knits should be cut with the grain line of the pattern along a lengthwise rib of the fabric. Sometimes the lengthwise rib is difficult to see, but it is there and must be observed.

4. Horizontally striped knits are cut so that the stripes are at right angles to the pattern grain line. Stripes should match along the seamlines.

5. Vertically striped knits are cut with the pattern grain line parallel to the edge of a stripe.

6. Striped or solid-color knits that stretch about the same amount in either direction can be cut with either the lengthwise or crosswise rib.

7. Striped knits can also be cut on the bias for special effects.

8. Do not let knit fabric hang over the table edge when cutting. This will stretch the fabric and cause construction and fitting problems.

9. Many knit fabrics have permanent creases along the fold. Re-fold your fabric to avoid these creases when pinning the pattern to the fabric. It is sometimes possible to use the crease down the center of the sleeve without affecting the look of the garment.

Solid-Color Fabric Layout. Re-fold the fabric, as illustrated, so that you avoid the permanent crease and have two folded edges instead of just one. Make sure that the folds are on a lengthwise rib of the knit. Pin the back and front pattern pieces in place with the tops facing one direction. The sleeves can be cut from the center section or below the body pieces. Remember to place the sleeve top in the same direction as the body pieces. Cut a left and right sleeve.

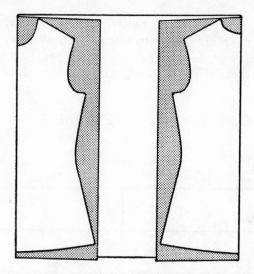

Striped-Fabric Layout. Cut only a single layer of fabric when working with a striped knit. It is easier to match stripes this way. The stripes should match at the lower corners of the pattern, at the underarm points, and at the shoulder points. These points should match on both back and front pattern pieces.

Cut the sleeves from the center section or from the area below the body pieces. Cut one sleeve at a time, matching the underarm point of the sleeve with the underarm point of the front pattern piece. Cut one sleeve with the printing right side up and one sleeve with the printing upside down so that you make a right and left sleeve.

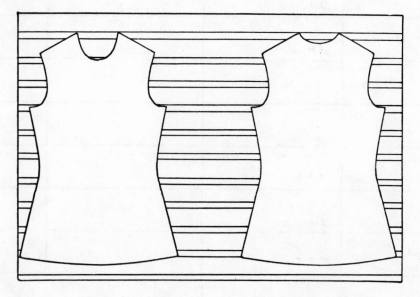

9 or 11

Matching stripes on a pattern with a bust dart will present a slightly different problem. Place the back and front pattern pieces on the fabric so that the lower corners match. The stripes will then match along the side seams to the dart line. The stripes will generally not match above the dart, but this will not be noticeable because it is in the underarm area.

Note: Sometimes striped knits will seem to be twisted out of shape after they have been pre-shrunk. Do not take the time to try to pull them back into shape — just work with them as they are. As long as you place your expanded pattern pieces straight on the stripes, you will not have to worry. Those crooked edges will take care of themselves. Matching stripes at seamlines is the important thing.

## FAMILY MEASUREMENT CHART

| Measurement | Name | Name | Name |
|---|---|---|---|
| | Mom | Laura | |
| Head Circumference | 22" | 20½ | |
| Neck Circumference | 13¾" | 12 | |
| Bust or Chest | 38" | 25½ | |
| Waist | 29½ | 21½ | |
| Raglan Sleeve Length | 29" | 24 | |
| Set-In Sleeve Length | 24¼" | 19½ | |
| Hip — 7" from Waistline | | 26¼ | |
| Hip — 9" from Waistline | 41½" | | |
| Crotch Depth | 10½" | 8½ | |
| Pants Length | 40" | 35 | |
| Knit Top Length | 23" | 16 | |
| Dress Length | | | |

Shoulder    5½"    4½

# SEWING FACTS

Sewing on knit fabric will take a slightly different technique from sewing with woven fabric. In fact, after you have sewn with knits for a while, you will probably not want to work with woven fabric very much. One of the main reasons for this is that knit fabric does not fray. Seam finishes are seldom required on knits, and we will take advantage of this fact in some of the techniques that are described later in the book. Another advantage of working with knits is that you will line very few. Linings, if desired, will be confined to coats and jackets, but they are not generally used in dresses or skirts. If you use a woven lining in a knit garment, you will lose the ease and comfort that made you select a knit in the first place. The doubleknits that you will be using for dresses, suits, and pants have enough bounce to keep their shape.

## YOUR SEWING MACHINE

Any sewing machine, from an old treadle to the most fancy new machine, will sew knits. The key to easy sewing is a well-oiled, clean machine. Knit fabric produces a lot of lint, so your machine should be cleaned very often. Machines with top-loading bobbins should be brushed out before every sewing session. A drop of oil in the raceway will make for a smoother running machine also. Take care of your sewing machine, and it will give you few problems.

The tension on the threads should be balanced so that the stitches lock in the middle of the fabric. Adjust the tension control if necessary.

## MACHINE NEEDLES

The needle in your sewing machine should always be sharp and fairly fine. A dull needle will break threads as it goes through the knit fabric and cause holes or runs in your garment before you even try it on. The size of the needle that is used on most knits is size 11. Smaller needles can be used on lingerie fabric and larger ones on heavy fabrics. A dull needle or one of improper size can cause your machine to skip stitches.

A new needle is now on the market that has a ball point. This needle is designed to push the fabric yarns aside rather than to go through them; thus it reduces the chance of holes and runs. Try this type of needle and see how you like it.

## PINS

Fine, sharp pins with large glass or plastic heads will be easier to use than regular pins. The large head is easier to find in bulky knit fabrics. Corsage pins also work very well with knits. There are ball-point pins on the market now for use with knit fabric.

Do not sew over pins. Pull them out of the fabric just before you come to them. Lightly hitting a pin with your machine needle is enough to take the point off and cause runs or holes in your fabric.

## SCISSORS

Knit fabric requires sharp scissors. Dull scissors will chew up your fabric and give you very tired hands. Do not use pinking shears on knits. These will cause many knit fabrics to fray.

## THREAD

There are many new threads on the market now that are suggested for use with knits. They are either all-polyester or a polyester core wrapped in cotton. These synthetic threads are strong and have some stretch.

Cotton mercerized thread can be used with all knits without any problems as long as you make a good knit seam.

## THE KNIT SEAM

A knit fabric is constructed so that it stretches in both crosswise and lengthwise directions. Seams in knit garments must be able to stretch with the fabric when stress is placed on them. If you do not provide for this, you will spend a lot of time repairing seams.

A knit seam can be made by one of two methods. The method that you choose will depend on the type of sewing machine you own.

Method 1. The first method, which can be used with all types of machines, involves stretching the fabric while it is being sewn. Use a stitch length of 9 or 10 stitches per inch. Anchor the fabric with one hand behind the presser foot to prevent it from pulling out from under the needle, and stretch it from the front. The threads will be slightly loose after the seam has been sewn, but will then be able to stretch out again when stress is placed on the seam.

Stretching the fabric while you are sewing will take a little bit of practice before you can get straight seams. Cut a few scraps of knit fabric and make some seam samples until you master the techinque. It is not hard but you will need some practice.

You will probably notice that the width of the seam allowance will become slightly less when the fabric is stretched. If you sew what looks like a 5/8-inch seam allowance on stretched fabric, you will have a seam allowance closer to ¾ inch when the fabric is relaxed. Keep this in mind as you sew the stretched fabric. Make the stretched seam about ½ inch wide, and it will then be closer to 5/8 inch when it is relaxed.

Method 2. Perhaps you are lucky enough to own a new Touch & Sew* sewing machine by SINGER or one of the new foreign-made sewing machines. These machines have either special stretch stitches built into their mechanisms or double cams, which form the stitches. These stitches utilize a back-and-forth motion, as well as a side-to-side motion, to produce a very strong seam with stretch.

The straight stretch stitch consists of three stitches forward and one or two stitches backwards. This series of stitches is then repeated. This process makes a very strong seam with built-in stretch. It is not necessary to stretch the fabric while using this stretch stitch.

Another special stretch stitch, straight-stitches and overcasts the edge of the seam allowance in one operation. It utilizes a side-to-side motion, as well as a back-and-forth motion. This overedge stitch is great to use on the narrow seam allowances that some knit fabrics and garments require. It is a real time-saver.

*A Trademark of THE SINGER COMPANY

A word of caution — the new stretch stitches are convenient to use and do make a strong knit seam, but they are difficult to undo if you should make a mistake or have a fitting problem Use them only after you are sure that the fitting problems are all taken care of.

Seam Width. Examine various ready-made knit garments, and you will notice that not all of the seams are of the same width. Some garments will have 5/8-inch seams that are pressed open, and others will have a very narrow seam with overcast edges. The width of the seam allowance is determined by the type of knit that is being used and sometimes by the type of garment that is being made.

Some knit fabrics cannot handle a pressed-open seam allowance. The fabric is so soft that the edges will roll up and make ridges along the seamline. This problem is solved by trimming the seam allowance to ¼ inch and then stitching the seam edges together.

The narrow seam allowance is also used for most knit shirts, tops, and children's clothes, regardless of the type of knit fabric that is used. It is better suited to these types of garments than the regular 5/8-inch seam allowance. It is also very strong because of the extra stitching.

Special knit patterns usually have only a ¼-inch seam allowance. Conventional patterns have the regular 5/8-inch seam allowance, which should be trimmed to ¼ inch when the narrow seam is indicated.

Three methods of making the narrow seam are described below.

1. Straight Stitch Machine: Do one row of straight stitching along the seamline, stretching the fabric as you sew. If you are working with just a ¼-inch seam allowance, you will then close the edges together with another row of straight stitching, stretching as you sew.

If your pattern has a 5/8-inch seam allowance, you will do the second row of stitching ¼ inch to the right of the first one. Stretch the seam as you sew, and then trim away the excess seam allowance.

2.  **Zig-Zag Machine:** Make one row of straight stitching along the seam line, stretching as you sew. Close the seam edges with a wide zig-zag stitch.

If your pattern has a 5/8-inch seam allowance, you should zig-zag close to the first line of stitching and then trim away the excess seam allowance.

**Note:** It is usually not necessary to stretch knit fabric when a zig-zag stitch is used because the stitch has plenty of stretch built into it. However, some lightweight knit fabrics need some extra support when they are zig-zagged. You will find it is easier to stitch them if the fabric is held taut as it goes under the presser foot. This prevents the fabric from being pulled down through the throat plate and will help eliminate skipped stitches.

3.  **New Stretch Stitch Machines:** For those of you who are the owners of these new sewing machines, there is a much quicker way to make a knit seam. Use the overedge stitch as you sew the ¼-inch seam, and the two rows of stitching will be done in one operation.

If your pattern has a 5/8-inch seam allowance, you will first use the overedge stitch along the seamline, and them trim away the excess seam allowance.

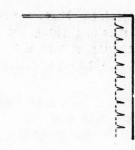

A regular 5/8-inch seam allowance is used when the knit fabric can be pressed open and remain that way. Most doubleknits can take this type of seam, and it is also the seam that is recommended for skirts and pants because it gives a much smoother line over the hips.

1. Straight Stitch Machine: If you are using a straight stitch machine, set the stitch length at 9 or 10 stitches per inch, and stretch the fabric as you sew. Press the seam allowance open.

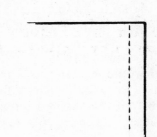

2. New Stretch Stitch Machines: Use the straight stretch stitch for your seam, and then press the seam allowance open. This is a very strong seam and has plenty of stretch for action garments.

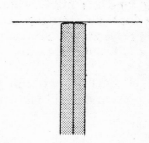

## PRESSING KNITS

Pressing is the secret of professional-looking garments in either knit or woven fabrics. Your pressing techniques are especially important when working with knits because some knits are quite resistant to being pressed and having seams flattened. It can be done with a little patience and work, and the result is most rewarding. Remember to press as you sew. Do not leave all the pressing to the last.

An Iron All sole-plate attachment for the iron makes pressing knits a breeze. It eliminates the need for a press cloth and lets you see what you are doing when pressing on the right side of the fabric.

Your most important tool when pressing knits is a good steam iron. Let the steam do the work. Do not use too much pressure, and always press with the lengthwise rib of the knit fabric. An up-and-down motion is better than a back-and-forth motion. Use a light touch and lots of moisture, and you will be surprised at the results.

A permanent crease can be made down the front of your pants if you use lots of moisture. Always use a press cloth when working on the right side of knit fabric, and moisten it if your steam iron does not provide enough moisture.

## INTERFACINGS, LININGS, AND INTERLININGS

These three items are not as necessary to the construction of knit garments as they are in woven-fabric garments. One reason is that knit garments use many neckline and armhole finishes that do not require facings and interfacings. Another is that knit garments, lined with woven fabric, lose the stretch of the knit, and this defeats your purpose in selecting a knit in the first place. Interlining is usually not necessary in knit garments because the fabric has plenty of body without it.

There will be occasions, however, when you will want to add some support to a neckline, collar, or lapel edge. I would recommend a piece of woven interfacing fabric that is cut on the bias for these areas. This will give extra firmness but still preserve some of the stretch. I have also found that press-on, non-woven interfacing is good to use in small details such as pocket flaps. This is easy to work with because it is bonded to the fabric.

Tricot (lingerie fabric) can also be used to provide some extra firmness to knit fabrics. Bond the tricot to the wrong side of the knit fabric, and then handle the two pieces as one. Use one of the bonding products that are available in fabric stores, and follow the instructions carefully. I have found that the secret of a good bond is plenty of steam. Use a moist press cloth if your steam iron is not up to par.

Buttonhole areas should be stabilized with a woven interfacing fabric before the buttonholes are made. Slip this interfacing piece between the two layers of knit, or bond it in place.

Always stitch on the interfacing side when you are attaching a piece of interfacing to a knit fabric. This will prevent the knit fabric from stretching out of shape during the stitching.

## HEMS

Hems in knit garments should have stretch in them just like the seams so that they can give with the fabric. This can be achieved by hand or by machine. The blind-hem stitch on your machine can be used to hem casual knit garments. This produces a hem with stretch because of the zig-zag stitch that is part of the blind-hem pattern. However, I would not recommend the use of this hem on your nicer knit garments. It tends to show a bit, and you want invisible hems on these clothes.

It is not necessary to turn under the raw edge of the hem as you do on lightweight woven fabrics. Knits are too bulky, and a ridge would show on the right side if you did. The cut edge of a knit will not ravel, so it does not have to be protected in this way. It does look nice if you do zig-zag over the hem edge.

Seam binding is not generally recommended for knit hems because it does not allow any give in the hem area and will often cause a ridge to show on the right side. Follow the instructions below for a nice knit hem.

The <u>Knit Hem</u>. Stitch around the edge of the hem with either a straight stitch or zig-zag. Pin the hem in place, and then fold it back as illustrated. Use a double thread and do a catch stitch between the hem edge and the garment. Catch just one thread of the fabric on each side with your hemming thread, and do not pull the threads tight. If you are right-handed, you will put your needle into the fabric to the left, but you will be hemming toward the right. If you are left-handed, your needle will go into the fabric to the right, but you will be hemming to the left. This technique creates the crossed effect.

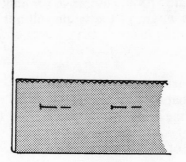

Press the edge of the hem carefully from the wrong side, but avoid pressing the top of the hem. This will produce a beautiful hem that will not show on the right side of the garment.

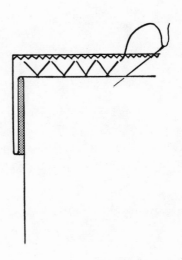

This same stitch can be done over the raw edge of the hem if the fabric tends to be loosely knit. If it is done loosely enough, the hem will show very little from the right side, and the hemming threads will help control the edge of the fabric. I like to use this technique on alpaca sweaters.

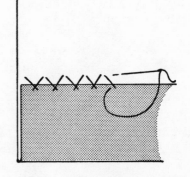

The Double Hem for Knits. Some bulky and heavy knit fabrics will require more support to the hem so that the weight of the fabric will not pull on the hem stitches and cause them to show.

A row of knit hem stitches will be placed halfway between the bottom and top edge of the hem. Then work a second row of knit hem stitches at the top edge of the hem.

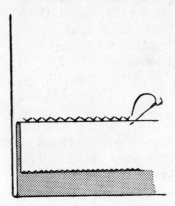

# HOW TO APPLY RIB TRIM

Talon's new Rib Trims are ideal for many of the neckline, sleeve, and edge finishes taught in Singer's knit course, "How to Sew Fashion Knits." The following instructions will help you discover how easy it is to use Rib Trims for your fashion-right wardrobe.

## HELPFUL HINTS

* To prevent stretching, work with trim on a flat surface.
* Eliminate facing pieces and hem allowances when trim is applied to armholes, necklines, and waistlines.
* When stitching with the trim side up, decrease the pressure on the presser foot.
* Evenly distribute fullness of fabric and trim. Divide both into quarters and pin first.
* Press trim lightly on the wrong side. Use a steam iron at a synthetic setting.

## NECKLINE AND SLEEVE APPLICATION

*Narrow Solid-Color Rib Trims*

1. Trim garment seam allowance to 1/4 inch.
2. The length of the ribbing should be the same as the body measurement. This measurement includes a 1/4-inch seam allowance.
3. Slash along one fold for about 2½ inches from each end of the ribbing piece. (Fig. 1 on page 30)
4. Stitch ribbing across ends with right sides together, leaving a 1/4-inch seam allowance. (Fig. 2)
5 Press the seam open with your fingers and fold the ribbing back in the original position with the right sides out.
6. Divide the ribbing and garment edge into four equal sections, and pin them together, matching quarter marks. (Fig. 3)
7. With trim side up, stitch 1/4 inch from the edge.

*Medium and Wide Tri-Color Rib Trims*

1. Trim garment seam allowance to 1/4 inch.
2. The length of the ribbing should be the same as the body measurement. This measurement includes a 1/4-inch seam allowance.
3. Form the ribbing into a circle by stitching the cut ends together, leaving a 1/4-inch seam allowance. (Fig. 4)
4. Finger-press the seam open, and hand-tack the ribbing seam allowances flat. (Fig. 5)
*Complete the application by following steps 6 and 7 above.*

## WAISTLINE APPLICATION

*Choose a pattern with a self-fabric waist insert or add the medium or wide ribbing to the bottom of a short jacket or knit top.*

1. Trim the waistline seam allowance to 1/4 inch.
2. Measure the ribbing against your body, stretching it until you get the look you want. Add seam allowances to this measurement.
3. Leave one seam open and apply ribbing to garment by dividing both ribbing and garment edges into four equal sections. Pin together and stitch.
4. Close seam or stitch zipper in place, making sure that the edges of the ribbing match across the seam line or zipper. (Fig. 6)

## BINDING

*Use narrow trim in a matching or contrasting color to bind necklines and sleeve and pocket edges. Seam allowances should be trimmed away from all edges to be bound.*

1. Measure the edge or edges to which the trim will be applied just as you would for any other trim. Purchase that amount.
2. Place trim 1/4 inch over edge of wrong side of fabric. Pin and baste, stretching ribbing slightly.
3. Straight-stitch, with fabric side up, close to the raw edge of the garment. (Fig. 7)
4. Turn ribbing to the right side, enclosing raw edge. Stretch outer edge of trim to accommodate curved areas. Pin and baste.
5. Straight-stitch close to the edge of the rib trim, as shown. When binding straight edges, stitch this row in the opposite direction from the first row of stitches. (Fig. 8)
6. After closing the seam left open for application of the trim, complete garment according to pattern instructions. Lightly press this seam open, and hand-tack the ribbing seam allowances flat. (Fig. 5)

**NOTE:** If the bound finish is going to be used with the exposed zipper at the neckline, butt the cut edges of the trim together and stitch the trim into a circle with a zig-zag stitch before applying it to the neckline. The zipper will then be positioned so that it ends at the top of the trim. (See page 53 for exposed zipper application.)

Fig. 1

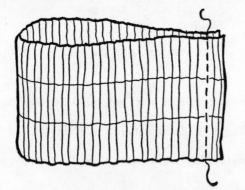

Fig. 2

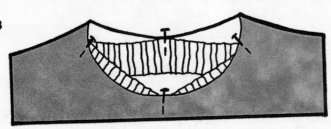

Fig. 3

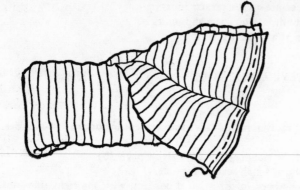

Fig. 4

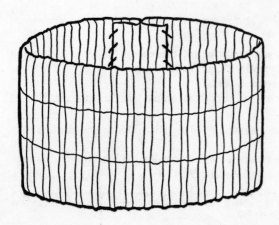

Fig. 5

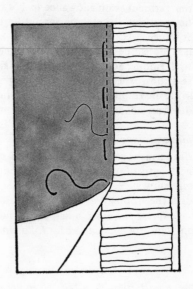

Fig. 6

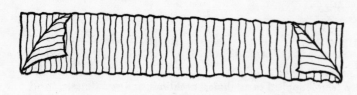

Fig. 7

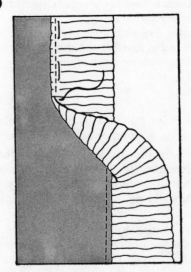

(Fig. 8)

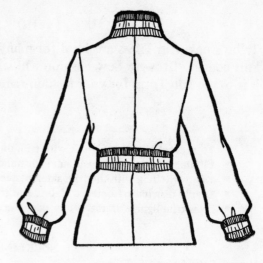

# THE BASIC KNIT TOP

The basic knit top is probably one of the easiest knit garments to make, so it is a good choice for your first project. Select either a conventional or special knit pattern that has a high, round neck and set-in sleeves. The neck opening will be finished with ribbing in the crew-neck, turtleneck, or mock turtleneck style. The techniques described in this section can be applied to knit tops for men, women, and children. It does not take long to make this type of top, and you will be very pleased with the results.

## BASIC NECKLINE FINISHES

First of all, you must select the proper size pattern and then decide which neckline finish you want your top to have. Choose from a crew-neck, turtleneck, or mock turtleneck finish. Special knit patterns usually have the different necklines marked, and some of the conventional patterns do also.

If you are working with a pattern that does not have the different necklines marked, you can make a few adjustments and then go ahead with the neckline finish you desire. Your pattern should have a high, round neckline to begin with.

Trim the seam allowance around the neck edge so that it is just ¼ inch wide. Use this neckline for a turtleneck or mock turtleneck finish.

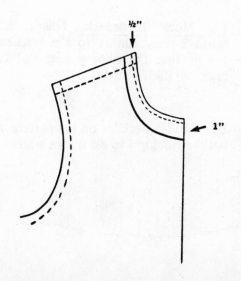

Draw a low neckline on the pattern back and front by following the illustration to the right. The new line is your cutting line, and there is a ¼-inch seam allowance below it. This neckline is used for a crew-neck finish.

You can use the same pattern for both the high and low neckline if you cut along the low neckline to within ½ inch of the center-front and center-back lines. Keep the small section up for a high neckline, and fold it down for a crew-neck.

FOR HIGH NECKLINE

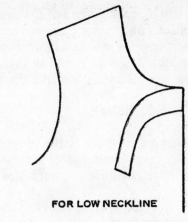

FOR LOW NECKLINE

Read through the material below so that you become familiar with the three basic neckline finishes and how they differ.

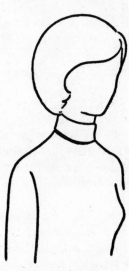

The Turtleneck. A turtleneck top is made from the high neckline on your pattern. A wide band of ribbing is sewn to the neck edge. The ribbing starts at the base of the neck, goes up the neck for approximately 2 inches, and then folds over on itself.

The ribbing is cut 9 to 10 inches wide.

The Mock Turtleneck. This neckline finish is very similar to the turtleneck except that the ribbing does not turn back on itself.

Use the high neckline on the pattern, and cut the ribbing 4 to 4½ inches wide.

The Crew-Neck. This variation of the knit top will use the crew or low neckline on the pattern. The ribbing starts about 1 inch below the base of the neck and ends at the base of the neck.

The ribbing is cut 3 inches wide for a crew-neck finish.

## PATTERN LAYOUT

Refer to the PATTERN FACTS section for pattern layout information. Remember to use an expanded pattern if you are working with a striped fabric. Cut out the fabric, set up the steam iron, thread the machine, and you are ready to sew.

## CONSTRUCTION STEPS

Follow the construction steps below to help you make your knit top. You will be surprised at how quickly it can be made.

The Shoulder Seam. The first seam to be sewn on your knit top is the shoulder seam. Make a narrow knit seam, using one of the methods described on page 23. Press the completed seam to one side.

Preparing the Ribbing. Cut a strip of ribbing that is wide enough to give you the desired neckline finish. Recommended widths for three neckline finishes are as follows: crew-neck, 3 inches; mock turtleneck, 4-4½ inches; and turtleneck, 9-10 inches. Then cut the ribbing open along one of the folds so that you have a long strip.

Note: Various ribbings have different amounts of stretch. The length that you need for one ribbing is not necessarily the length that you will need for another ribbing. Always measure to be sure that you have enough to go over the head.

First, measure your head circumference and neck circumference. Fold the ribbing strip in half lengthwise and mark the neck measurements with a pin.

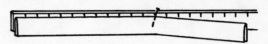

Stretch this marked amount to see whether it will extend out to the head measurement plus ½ inch.

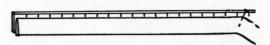

If it can stretch that far without causing runs in the ribbing, you can use that amount of ribbing around the neck opening. If it stretches beyond the head measurement, you can then use 1 to 1½ inches less ribbing. In this case you should hold the adjusted length in position around your neck to make sure that it will not be too tight.

Place the right sides of the measured ribbing together, and straight-stitch across the narrow ends with a ¼-inch seam allowance. Press the seam allowance open with your fingers, and fold the ribbing so that you have a double tube of ribbing with the right sides out.

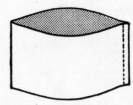

Divide the ribbing into four equal sections by placing one pin at the seamline and another directly opposite. Fold the ribbing in half so that these two pins touch. Place another pin at each new fold. It is important that you be accurate in this quartering process.

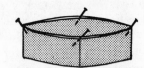

Applying the Ribbing. Quarter the neck edge of the knit top by first placing pins at the center front and the center back.

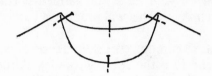

Re-fold the top so that these two pins are together. Run the neck edges out parallel to each other until you come to the fold. Mark these new folds with pins, and your neck opening will look like the illustration to the right. Note that the shoulder seams are not quarter marks.

Turn the knit top inside out and slip the prepared ribbing down into the neck opening, right sides together. Place the ribbing seam at the center back. Match up the quarter marks, and pin the ribbing to the neck opening at these points.

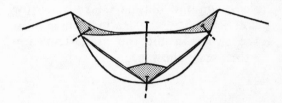

Place the ribbing on the top and the neck opening on the bottom when you begin to sew. Start your stitching at the center back. Stretch the ribbing to fit each quarter section, and sew around the neck opening, using one of the narrow-knit-seam methods.

Press the neck area from the wrong side so that the seam allowance goes down into the shirt. Let your steam iron shrink out any puckering.

The back of the crew-neck can be top-stitched to help keep the seam allowance in place. Use a regular straight stitch for this stitching. Do not topstitch a turtleneck or mock turtleneck finish.

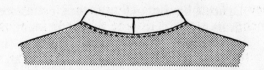

Sleeves. The sleeves in casual knit tops can be stitched in before the underarm seam is sewn. This is a very quick and easy method. However, I would suggest that you use the conventional set-in sleeve method on your nicer knit garments. The sleeve is sewn into the arm opening after the underarm seam has been sewn. This will produce a better-fitting sleeve in these garments.

Make sure that the shoulder seam point is marked on the top of your sleeve by either a notch or a small clip into the seam allowance. Also mark any notches or small circles found on both sleeve and arm openings. These marks will help you distribute the sleeve ease evenly.

Pin the sleeve into the arm opening, right sides together, matching all the marks. Place the fabric under the presser foot with the arm opening on the top and the sleeve on the bottom. Make a narrow knit seam. Stretch the arm opening to fit the sleeve in the cap area. Trim any excess seam allowance.

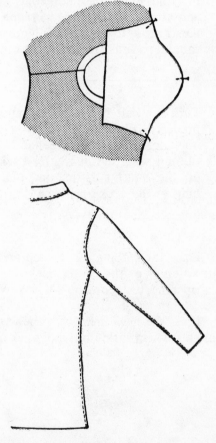

The Side Seam. Pin the side seams together, matching stripes, if you are working with a striped fabric. Start your knit seam at the bottom of the knit top, stitching through the underarm area and out to the edge of the sleeve. Trim the excess seam allowance, if necessary, and press to one side.

Finishing the Knit Top. The sleeves and bottom edge of the knit top can be hemmed by machine or by hand. Follow the instructions in the SEWING FACTS section.

The sleeve and bottom edge of the knit top can also be finished with a strip of ribbing. This is a quick method and a finish that you will find on many ready-made garments.

Sleeve: Trim the hem allowance. Measure around your arm at the point where the sleeve ends. Cut a 4-inch-wide strip of ribbing that is ½ inch less than your arm measurement.

Sew the ribbing together as though you were making a neckline trim. Divide the sleeve opening and sleeve trim in half, and pin the trim in place, right sides together. It works better if the sleeve is inside out at this point. Stretch the ribbing to fit, and stitch with a narrow knit seam.

Bottom Edge: Ribbing can be applied to the bottom edge of knit tops if they are not tapered at the waistline. This finish works well on a straight shirt.

Measure around the bottom edge. Cut a 4-to-5-inch-wide strip of ribbing that is 4 inches less than the bottom measurement

Sew the ribbing together as though you were making a neckline trim. Divide the bottom edge and ribbing into four equal sections. Pin them with right sides together, matching the quarter marks. Sew with a narrow knit seam.

# PANTS

Knit pants are fun to make and a joy to wear. Once you have adjusted your pattern to give you a custom fit, you will be able to whip up a pair of knit pants in one hour. What could be quicker, and who doesn't need more pants?

When selecting material for pants, look for fabric that will hold its shape. This is important for the knee and seat areas. Doubleknits are most satisfactory and easy to care for. Polyesters are very attractive and practical because they are washable. They come in a variety of textures and patterns, so you can have both dressy and casual pants that can be machine-washed and dried. Wool works up easily and is very handsome, but it must be dry-cleaned. The doubleknit acrylics are used for pants, also, but they should be dried carefully to prevent fuzz balls and excessive shrinkage. Doubleknit nylon was one of the first fabrics used for knit pants, and it is very comfortable and inexpensive. It will not keep a crease, however, and it will bag in the knee and seat areas. It is useful for Bermuda shorts and children's pants, and is comfortable for activities that require a lot of action but do not require a "just pressed" look. Pants made of doubleknit nylon can usually be made one size smaller than your other doubleknits because the fabric has so much stretch. Doubleknit cotton and cotton blends can be used for shorts and Bermudas, but they will bag in the knee area in long pants. It is important that you pre-shrink all knit fabrics used for pants.

## THE PATTERN

You should have no trouble finding a pattern for a pair of knit pants. All of the special knit pattern series have a pants pattern, and now there are many conventional patterns available that are designed just for knits. These patterns give you the pull-on style with the elastic waistband. They do not require darts or a zipper opening. If you prefer your pants to have darts and a separate waistband, you can use a regular pattern and, by following the instructions in the SKIRT section of this book, apply a separate waistband. These will also slip on over your hips with no side opening.

The following information describes a pattern for knit pants. You can use this information to help you alter your pattern so that your pants will fit you properly.

1. There should be a pattern extension of at least 1½ inches above the waistline. This allows for a turned-over waistband to encase the elastic.

2. The pants pattern should measure 1 inch larger than your largest hip measurement.

3. The waist opening should be at least 4 inches larger than your actual waistline measurement. If your hip measurement is more than 11 inches larger than your waist measurement, you should allow an extra 1 or 2 inches of ease in the waist area.

Buy your pants pattern according to your hip measurement. The waistline can be adjusted very easily if your measurement is different from the pattern's.

Check your pattern to see what seam width has been allowed. Conventional patterns and some special knit pattern will have a 5/8-inch seam allowance. Some of the special knit patterns allow only a ¼-inch seam allowance.

A 5/8-inch seam allowance is recommended for knit pants if the fabric you have selected will hold a press. This seam allowance will give you a very smooth line over the hips. Use the narrow seam allowance only when the fabric tends to roll and will not press flat. Adjust your pattern, if you do not have the wide seam allowance, by adding to the sides.

## BASIC PATTERN ALTERATIONS

Pattern companies allow different amounts of ease in their pants patterns, so it is a good idea to compare your body measurements with the pattern measurements, and adjust the pattern where it is necessary. Remember not to include the seam allowances when you are measuring the pattern.

The Crotch Depth. Tie a string around your waist and sit up straight on a flat surface. Place the end of a tape measure at the string and bring it down over the hip curve, under the body, to the flat surface. Add 1 inch to this measurement for your crotch depth.

Check the pattern crotch depth by measuring the distance from the waist-line mark to the deepest part of the crotch. This measurement should be taken on the front pattern piece. Draw a horizontal line across the pattern piece to help you measure this depth if your pattern does not already have a line drawn. Follow the illustration at the right as a guide. The pattern crotch depth should equal your crotch depth measurement with the 1 inch added. Alter the pattern if necessary.

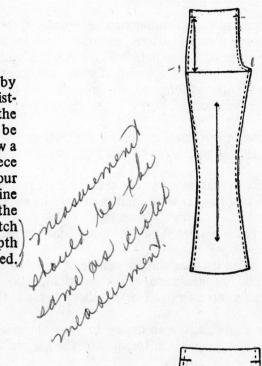

*measurement should be the same as crotch measurement.*

Add depth by slashing the pattern at the alteration line and spreading the two pieces apart the needed amount.

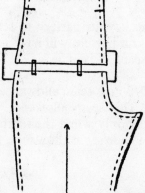

Subtract depth by folding the pattern along the alteration line and removing the excess depth.

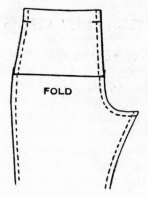

Alter both the back and the front pattern pieces the same amount.

The Waistline. The finished waist of the pattern should be 4 to 6 inches larger than your waist measurement. Many of the conventional patterns allow too much ease in the waist. These patterns should be altered before you pin them to your fabric.

Determine how much should be removed from the waist area by adding 4 to 6 inches to your actual waist measurement and then subtracting this amount from the pattern waist measurement. The difference is the excess that must be removed from the waistline of the pattern.

Divide this number by 6 and remove that amount from each side of the center back seam the front side seam, and the back side seam. More can be removed in the final fitting, if necessary.

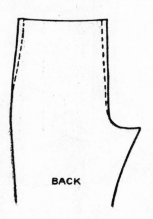

BACK

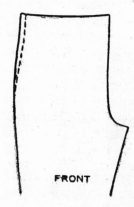

FRONT

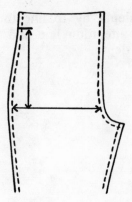

The <u>Hipline</u>. Measure the largest part of your hips, and determine how far this measurement falls below your waistline. Locate your hip on the pattern by measuring down from the waistline mark. Now measure the pattern width at this point. Remember not to include the seam allowances in this measurement. Measure both back and front pattern pieces and double the number so that you get the full hipline measurement.

The pattern should measure 1 inch more than your actual hipline measurement. Alter the pattern pieces along the side seams if there is a small change to be made. Make a vertical fold down the pattern piece if there is a large change. Alter both pattern pieces an equal amount.

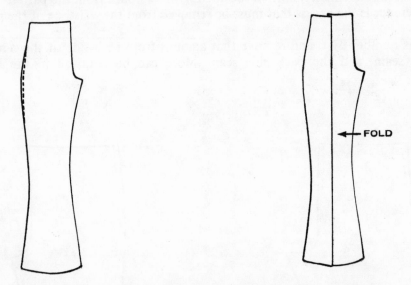

← FOLD

The <u>Rise</u>. If you are round in the front or round behind, you will probably want to allow more fabric at the center front and/or the center back to compensate for this. If you are in doubt about needing this additional fabric, it is recommended that you add it at this stage, and then check it again in the final fitting. If you do not need it, you can trim it away. But, if you do find it necessary for a good fit, you will be glad that you allowed the extra fabric.

Add up to an inch at the top of the center-front and/or center-back seam. Taper the line to the side seam. The amount that you need will be checked in the final fitting.

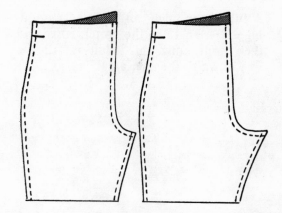

The Length. Decide how long you want your pants to be, and alter the pattern accordingly. Remember that wide-leg pants are worn longer than straight-leg pants. Allow 1½ to 2 inches for the hem.

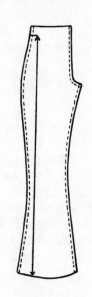

Measure your body from the waistline down to the point where you want your pants to end. Measure your pants pattern from the waistline to the hemline, and adjust the pattern by cutting and spreading, or by folding.

The Crotch Curve. Lengthen or shorten the crotch curve, if necessary, by adding to or subtracting from the inside leg seam. If you find the back of your pants pulling when you sit down, you probably need to lengthen your back curve a bit. If you are very flat in front and in back, you may need to shorten both the front and the back curves. The need for this alteration generally shows up in the first fitting.

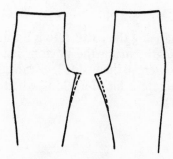

A full upper thigh can be fitted by adding extra length to the crotch curve and then continuing this addition all the way down to the knee area.

Leg Styles. If you have only a straight-leg pattern available, you can adjust the width of the leg for different styles. Straight-legs and stovepipes measure 18 to 21 inches around the bottom. Flared or belled legs measure 23 to 26 inches. If you cannot decide how wide you want your pants to be, you can measure a pair of ready-mades, or get the information from the back of a conventional pattern envelope.

Use the following instructions to help you change the style of your pattern.

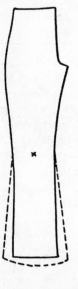

Measure from your waist to your knee, and mark the length on your pattern. Any flare will begin at the knee and extend an equal distance on each side. Decide how much extra is needed for your new style, and then add ¼ of that amount to each leg seam. Draw the bottom line as a curve rather than a straight line when making wide legs.

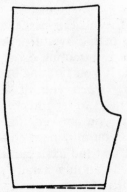

When changing the pattern to a Bermuda shorts length, make the bottom leg line ½ inch lower at the inside leg seam. This will eliminate a hiked-up look when you wear the shorts.

## PATTERN LAYOUT

Fold your fabric in half, using a lengthwise rib to help you fold it on-grain. Pin the pattern pieces to the fabric, using a "with nap" layout, and make sure that the grain line of the pattern is parallel to a lengthwise rib.

Solid-color fabrics can be cut double. Striped fabrics should be cut from a single layer, so that you can match the stripes accurately.

When cutting a single layer of fabric, you must be sure that you cut a left and right front and a left and right back. Do this by cutting one pants front with the pattern printing right side up, and the other pants front with the printing on the underside. Use the same procedure when cutting the pants back.

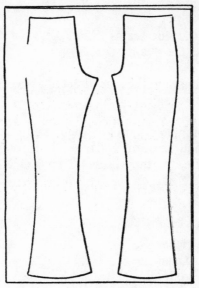

## ORDER OF CONSTRUCTION

Front crease
Side seams
In-seams
Back crease
Crotch seam
String fit
Elastic waistband
Hems

The Front Crease. Set the creases in the front of the pants legs before you sew any seams. Fold the leg in half, wrong sides together, and match the pants leg edges. The crease extends straight up the leg front to the waistline. A sharp crease can be made by using a moist pressing cloth and fairly warm iron. Never place the iron directly on the right side of the fabric.

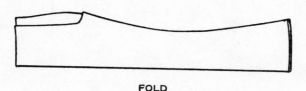

FOLD

A double needle can be used at this point to stitch along the crease line, if you wish. Spread the pants leg out flat with the right side up, and stitch down the center crease line with matching thread.

A sharper stitched crease can be made by stitching along the edge of the crease while the pants leg is still folded. I would recommend that you do this after the pants have been completed. The stitching can then go through the completed hem, and keep it very sharp.

If you prefer no creases at all, go on to the next step.

The Side Seams. Pin and sew the side seams. First, press the seam in the closed position in order to embed the stitches, and then press the steam open.

The In-Seam. Pin and sew the in-seam. Press as directed above. A sleeveboard is very useful to slip into the pants leg when you press this seam.

The Back Crease. Turn the completed pants leg right side out, and set the back crease. Fold the pants leg along the front crease, and smooth it flat on the ironing board. The side seam and the in-seam should be directly on top of each other. Press the back crease only up to the crotch area.

The Crotch Seam. Have one pants leg inside out and one pants leg right side out. Slip one inside the other so that the right sides are together. Place some pins at the in-seam, in the crotch curve, and at the top of the pants. Stitch together with one long seam. If you are using a simple straight stitch, as opposed to a straight stretch stitch, you must stretch the fabric quite firmly as you stitch around the crotch curve. This will produce the stretchy seam that is needed in this area.

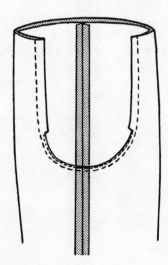

Trim the seam to ¼ inch in the curved area, and then zig-zag or straight stitch the edges together. Press the remaining seam allowance open.

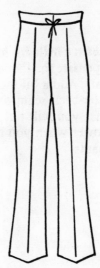

The String Fit. Try on your pants and tie a string snugly around your waist to hold them up. Stand in front of a mirror, and pull the pants up all around the waist until you have a smooth fit. Mark the waistline of your pants by putting a row of pins directly below the string.

If you have taken all your measurements properly and adjusted the pattern correctly, you will have at least 1½ inches of fabric above the pins. Trim any fabric in excess of the 1½ inches, and trim your paper pattern to correspond to the new cutting line. This procedure gives you a pair of knit pants with a custom fit, and eliminates the need for fitting your next pair of pants.

Fitting Problems. Some of you may run into a few fitting problems at this point. The information found below should help you overcome some of them. The other problems can usually be solved by taking in or letting out seams.

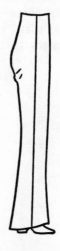

Problem 1: Sometimes you will find some bagginess right under the seat. This can be helped by taking a dart across the lower hip area of the back pattern piece.

Slash the pattern back, as indicated in Figure 1, from the center-back edge out to, but not through, the side edge. Overlap the slash ½ inch or slightly more, if needed. Figure 2. Tape in place, and then redraw and trim the overlapped edge at the center back so that it is even. Now recut the back of the pants to fit the altered pattern.

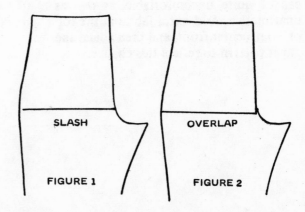

SLASH          OVERLAP

FIGURE 1       FIGURE 2

The crotch can be sewn a little bit lower, if necessary, to compensate for the length taken out by the dart. Add a bit more at the top of the center-back seam on the paper pattern so that you will not have to sew the crotch lower when you make your next pair of pants.

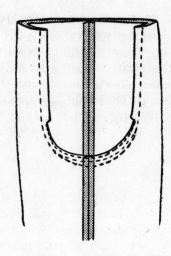

Problem 2: Sometimes you will have vertical wrinkles in the front-crotch area. This may result from the pants being too short at the center front seam, or having more fabric than necessary in the front crotch area.

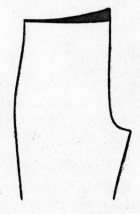

If the center-crotch seam is too short, the pants will pull in the crotch and this can be quite uncomfortable, as well as unattractive. Add extra fabric at the top of your center front, and then adjust the paper pattern to reflect this change.

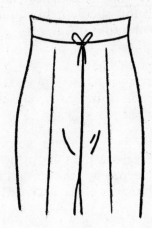

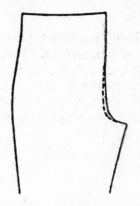

Perhaps your pants are not pulling but you still have wrinkles. Try your pants on inside out, and pin the crotch seam wider until you get rid of the extra fabric that is causing the problem. Sew a new seam, being careful not to make the crotch curve any lower. Then adjust your paper pattern to correspond to the new crotch curve.

The Elastic Waistband. Cut a strip of ¾-inch-wide pants elastic to fit snugly around the waist plus ½ inch. Join it into a circle with a ½-inch overlap. Stitch the overlap securely, and divide the elastic into four equal sections and mark.

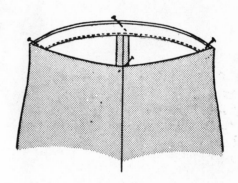

Pin the elastic to the inside of the waistline, matching each mark with a seam. Position the elastic so that the edge is 1/8 inch below the fabric edge. The elastic should be completely below the top edge of the pants. Stitch, using a wide zig-zag stitch, along the lower edge of the elastic, stretching the elastic to fit the fabric as you stitch.

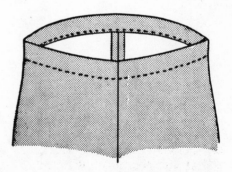

Turn the elastic and fabric once to the inside of the pants so that the elastic is completely covered by the fabric. Stitch as before but along the fabric and elastic edges and through the garment, stretching the elastic as you stitch. The straight stretch stitch may be used instead of a wide zig-zag stitch.

The Elastic Casing. Instead of stitching the elastic into the waistband, you can enclose it in an elastic casing. Cut a strip of pants elastic to fit snugly around your waist plus ½-inch for an overlap.

Leave a ¾-inch opening ¼ inch below the top of the center back seam. Fold the waist of the pants down 1¼-inch to the inside. Pin at 3-inch intervals. Stitch ¼ inch from the cut edge, stretching as you sew, or use a narrow zig-zag stitch.

Using a large safety pin, thread the elastic through the opening in the casing. Pull both ends of the elastic out through the opening, overlap, and stitch securely.

Distribute the fullness evenly around the waist and place pins on either side of each pants seam. Stitch in the seam groove of each seam, through the pants fabric and elastic. This will prevent the elastic from twisting in the casing.

# THE SHELL

A tailored or casual shell to be worn with your pants, skirts, and suits can be made from knit fabric. Select a conventional pattern that gives you the desired style, or choose a basic shell pattern from one of the special knit series. The shell can have a sleeve or be sleeveless. Use a pattern with a dart if you are working with a doubleknit fabric and want a more tailored look. Apply one of the neckline and armhole trims that are described below for a quick finish.

The zipper opening that is used in the shell does not require a center-back seam. It is the exposed zipper that you see in many ready-to-wear knit garments. If the pattern you are using has a center-back seam, you can fold it out of the way, and then place the pattern piece on a fabric fold.

## DART RELOCATION

Shell patterns with a bust dart should be checked to make sure that the location of the dart is right for your figure. Usually, some alteration in the bust area is necessary. It is simple to do and will greatly improve the fit of your garment. This information will apply to your dress patterns also.

Darts should be directed toward the high point of your bust and stop 1 inch short of it. The angle and length of the dart should be adjusted to fit your bustline.

Follow these steps for a quick pattern adjustment.

1. Determine the "drop" of your bust by measuring from the middle of your shoulder seam to the high point of your bust. Place a dot on your pattern that corresponds to this measurement.

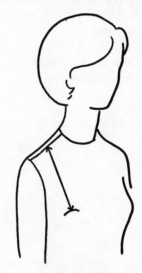

2. Determine the "separation" of your bust by measuring between the high points. Use ½ of that measurement, and locate it on your pattern by measuring in from the center-front line.

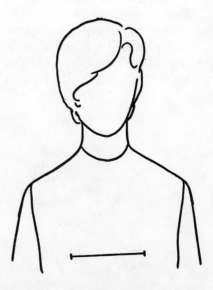

If the two dots are not in the same place, move the bust "drop" dot over until it is directly above or below the "separation" dot. This will now mark the high point of your bust.

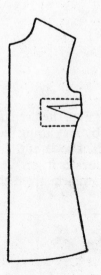

3. Check the direction of the bust dart and see if it is going toward the high-point mark. Do this by placing the edge of a ruler along the fold line of the dart and let it extend past the bust dot. You may find that the dart is either too high or too low for your bustline.

If you need to adjust the bust dart, it can be done quite easily by cutting a box around the dart and raising or lowering the whole dart as needed. Tape the dart in the proper place and fill in the gap with an extra piece of pattern paper.

The dart should be sewn short of the high point. End the dart about 1 inch behind the high point for pattern sizes 14 and smaller. Larger size patterns should have the dart end about 1½ to 2 inches behind the high point. Check the length of the dart to see if it is right for you. Alter the dart length if necessary.

Place a ruler along the center fold line of the dart and extend it to the bust dot. Using the above information, either lengthen or shorten the dart. Perhaps no alteration is needed for you, and you can use the pattern as it is.

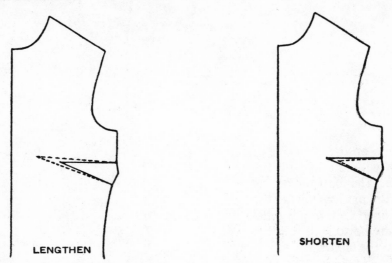

LENGTHEN    SHORTEN

It is a good idea to check the bust darts on all the patterns that you use to see if they will give you the fit that you want. Another thing to keep in mind when you are relocating darts is that you should wear the same bra when you take your measurements as you will wear under the finished garment. You are probably aware that different bra styles, and an old or new bra, can change your high-point location.

## PATTERN LAYOUT

Place your pattern pieces on the fabric, using a "with nap" layout. Use a lengthwise rib for a grain line. Solid-color fabric can be cut double, but it is best to cut striped fabric from a single layer.

## THE EXPOSED ZIPPER

This type of zipper is sewn in the center back of a shell or other garment that has been cut without a center-back seam. It is sewn in before any other seams are made.

You will need a 7- or 9-inch zipper that has been pre-shrunk, and a piece of stay fabric that measures 3 inches wide and 2 inches longer than the zipper. Stay fabric is a woven underlining fabric. It should be fairly lightweight and firmly woven. The color does not matter since it will not show on the completed garment. Pre-shrink all stay fabric.

Draw a line that is the length of the zipper plus the width of the neckline seam allowance down the center of the stay fabric.

Lightly press a 5- or 6-inch crease along the center back of the shell. This is a guideline for centering the zipper. Place the zipper on the crease with the top of the zipper teeth at the neck seamline. Mark the bottom of the zipper teeth with a pin.

Place the stay fabric on the right side of the garment back with the line on the center-back crease. The bottom of the line should be at the pin that marks the bottom of the zipper. Stitch along the drawn line from the bottom to the top, using 12 stitches to the inch.

Now stitch a long box around the center line so that it will be ¼ inch wide when finished.

Slash down the center line, cutting to within ½ inch of the bottom and then cut into the corners, making a wedge.

Turn all the stay fabric to the wrong side, and press so that none of it shows on the right side. You now have a neatly faced slot.

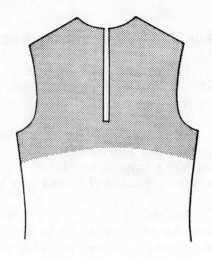

Slip the zipper into the slot, and pin it in place, making sure that the metal stopper at the bottom of the teeth is exposed. Lift the bottom part of the garment until you find the ends of the zipper tape and the wedge. Stitch across the base of the wedge, securing it to the zipper tape.

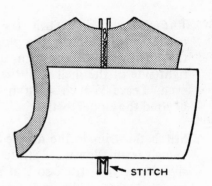

← STITCH

Unpin one side of the zipper, and fold back the side of the garment until you see the zipper and the original stitching line. Use a zipper foot, and stitch the garment to the zipper tape by sewing up this stitching line. Keep the cut edge of the shell parallel to the zipper tape. You should be able to just see this through the stay fabric. Stitch from the bottom to the top.

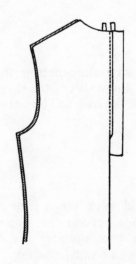

Unpin the other side of the zipper, fold back the other side of the shell, and stitch the zipper in from the bottom up. It is important that both lines of stitching go in the same direction.

Now sew the shoulder seams together and press them open.

## NECKLINE AND ARMHOLE TRIMS

The neckline and armhole of your shell can be trimmed in various ways. Try some of the methods below and see which ones you like. They are all quite easy and make a professional-looking garment.

The Edge Trim. The edge trim is an attractive finish that can be used around neck and arm openings and also along the edges of suit jackets and around hems. It is made of a matching or contrasting strip of knit fabric that is used to bind the cut or folded edge of a garment. All seam allowances should be trimmed from the areas that will be finished with the edge trim.

Cut the trim strip 3 inches wide from either a matching or a contrasting fabric. Cut the strip across the width of the fabric so that it has a good amount of stretch. Ribbing can be used for edge trim also. You will need enough length to go around the neck and armhole edges

The Neck Trim: Turn the garment inside out and unzip the zipper. Place the right side of the trim against the right side of the shell with the cut edges even. Leave ½ inch of trim extending beyond the zipper teeth.

Stitch the trim to the neck edge with a ½-inch seam allowance. Stretch the trim slightly as you stitch so that it will follow the curve of the neck edge. Leave ½ inch of trim extending beyond the other end of the neck edge.

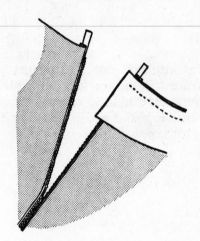

Correct any unevenness in the seam allowance before doing the final stitching. This is important because the width of the seam allowance will determine the width of the finished trim. If your seam is crooked, the trim will be uneven.

Fold back the ½ inch of trim that extends beyond the zipper. Lightly press the trim up over the seam allowance, using a steam iron.

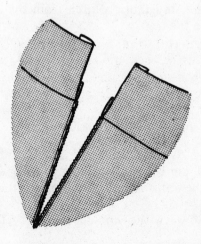

Fold the trim over the seam allowance and to the inside of the shell. Catch the trim in place by carefully stitching in the seam groove that is formed by the joining of the trim and the neck edge. Shorten your stitch length to about 20 stitches to the inch, and they will be buried in the fabric and never be seen.

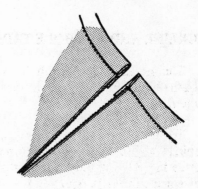

Cut away the excess trim on the inside of the garment. You can trim close to the stitching line and not have to worry about the stitches coming undone because knits do not fray.

The Armhole Trim: Place the right side of the trim against the right side of the armhole with the cut edges even. The narrow edge of the trim should be even with the side edge of the shell.

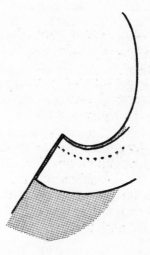

Stretch the trim slightly in the curved areas as you stitch it with a ½-inch seam allowance. Check the evenness of the seam allowance, and correct it if necessary. Cut the trim even with the other edge of the armhole.

Press the trim over the seam allowance, and then sew the side seams of the shell. Make sure that the trim seamlines match on the right side after the side seams have been sewn.

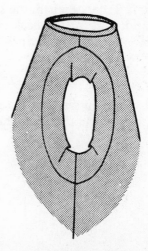

Fold the trim to the inside of the shell, and catch it in place by stitching in the seam groove on the right side. Cut away the excess trim.

This same technique can be used around the edge of a short or long sleeve. Stitch the trim in place before the underarm seam is sewn. The trim does not have to be stretched as it is being sewn when it is used on a straight edge such as a sleeve.

Piping Trim. A narrow piping trim can be applied to neck and arm openings of your shell also. It can be of the same or a contrasting fabric. The seam allowance of the neck and arm opening should be trimmed to ¼ inch.

Cut the trim strip across the stretch of the fabric and 1¼ inches wide. Cut enough to go around the neck and arm openings. Press over one of the long edges of the trim 3/8 inch so that the wrong sides are together.

The Neck Trim: Place the right side of the small section against the right side of the neck edge. The folded edge is going down into the garment — the wide section of trim should be up beyond the neck edge. Leave ½ inch of trim extending beyond the zipper teeth.

Make a seam 1/8 inch from the edge of the trim fold, catching the trim to the garment opening.

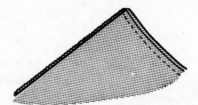

Fold under the ½ inch at the zipper, and press the trim to the wrong side of the garment. Catch the free edge of the trim with a row of topstitching or hand stitching on the wrong side.

The Armhole Trim: Prepare the strip of trim as directed above. Position it around the arm opening just as you did for the neck edge. The narrow edge of the trim should be even with the side edge of the shell. Stitch the trim in place.

Stitch the underarm seam of the shell up through the trim. Fold the trim down into the inside and topstitch or hand-stitch around the arm opening to keep it in place.

<u>Rib Trim</u>. Ribbing can be used to trim the arm openings of sleeveless shells also. First, trim the seam allowance around the arm opening to ¼ inch. You will now be adding an extra 1 inch of trim, so you must trim all around the arm opening 1 inch so that it can accommodate the extra trim.

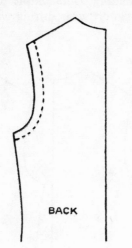

BACK

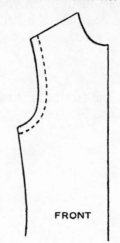

FRONT

Cut a strip of ribbing 2½ inches wide and 2 to 3 inches smaller than the arm opening. Join it together as though you were making a neck band. Fold it over double with the wrong sides together, and divide it into four equal sections. Divide the arm opening into four equal sections. Turn the shell inside out, and slip the prepared ribbing into the arm opening. Pin the quarter marks together, stretch the ribbing to fit, and make a narrow knit seam.

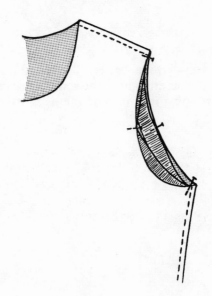

Press the trim from the wrong side so that the seam allowances go out into the shell.

**HEMS**

Finish your shell with the knit hem or choose any of the other hems described in the MORE ZIPPERS AND TRIMS section. The mock edge hem looks very nice with the edge trim around the neck and arm openings.

## THE TANK TOP

A tank top can be made from your shell pattern by making some simple pattern adjustments. These tops can be made in about a half an hour and are great to wear during warm weather. Use a pattern with or without a dart.

Lower the back and front of the pattern the desired amount.

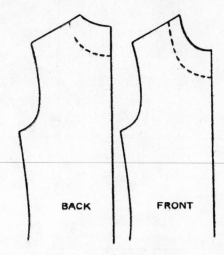

You will have a better fit around the neck if you straighten the shoulder seam by dropping it ¼ inch at the neck edge.

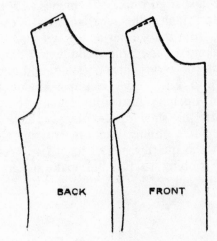

The arm opening can also be made wider by following the illustration at the right.

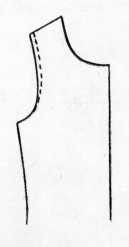

Sew the shoulder and side seams of the tank top. Finish the neck and arm edges by turning them under ½ inch and then topstitching. Use a straight stitch, a zig-zag, or a double needle for a quick finish. Two rows of topstitching often looks better than just one row.

Neckline and armhole trim, such as piping or edge trim, can also be used on the tank top.

# SKIRTS

Skirts are almost as much fun to make as pants. There is no limit to the styles that can be made from knit fabric. Straight skirts, flared skirts, pleated skirts, and even circle skirts come out beautifully. Doubleknits are the best fabrics for skirts, though, because they hold their shape and will not sit out. You will sometimes see skirts made from a sweater knit, and these are pretty also.

## THE PATTERN

Select either a conventional or a special knit skirt pattern. Compare body and pattern measurements, and adjust the pattern if necessary. Skirts made from firm doubleknit fabric should have about 1½ inches of ease through the hip area. If you are using a very stretchy knit, you will need only 1 inch or less of ease. The ease problem can easily be adjusted on the side seams before any waistband finishing is done.

Use a 5/8-inch seam allowance on your skirt patterns. A smooth line is achieved over the hips if the seam is pressed open. Add to the seam allowance if your pattern has only ¼ inch allowed.

## THE STRAIGHT SKIRT WITH A WAISTBAND

Any conventional pattern that fits you well can be used for this skirt, or you may wish to use a special knit pattern that includes darts and a separate waistband. Again, let's take some measurements to ensure a proper fit. The skirt should be 1½ inches larger than your widest hip measurement. This ease is needed to prevent the skirt from "cupping" under your buttocks. This is the recommended amount of ease for a doubleknit, but if you are using a very stretchy fabric, all of that ease may not be required.

The waistline of your skirt should be 1 to 2 inches larger than your actual waistline measurement. This skirt is going to pull up over your hips, so it's a good idea to try on the skirt before you apply the waistband to see whether it stretches enough.

Not everyone can wear this type of skirt, If your hips are more than 11 or 12 inches larger than your waist, you will probably need a zipper opening for a proper fit.

Assembling the Skirt. Sew the darts on your skirt, and press them toward the center of the body. Start the stitching line at the wide end of the dart and taper to nothing at the narrow end. If you continue stitching after you come off the edge of the fabric, you will knot the threads. Never backstitch at the end of a dart.

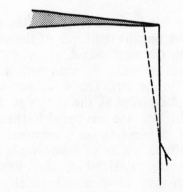

Stitch the side seams of the skirt, and press them open carefully. Now try on your skirt for a fitting. Tie a string around your waist, and stand in front of a mirror while you adjust the skirt. The skirt should hang from your waistline so that the side seams are at right angles to the floor. If the side seams swing to the front or back, you have a fitting problem at the waistline or hipline. Adjust the skirt at the waistline until the side seams hang straight. Place a row of pins just below the string to mark your waistline.

There should be a 5/8-inch width of fabric above the pin line for a seam allowance. If there is more than this amount on your skirt, you should trim the excess so that you have just the amount needed for a waistline seam. Trim your paper pattern to correspond to the changes you have made. Now you are ready to apply the waistband. Remember that this waistband can also be used on your knit pants.

The Waistband Application. Across the stretch of the fabric, cut a waistband that is 4 inches wide and 2 inches larger than your waistline measurement. Place the right sides together, and stitch with a ½-inch seam.

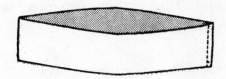

Quarter the waistband, quarter the skirt top, and pin the right side of the waistband to the right side of the skirt. The skirt will be easier to work with if it is turned inside out. The waistband seam should be placed at the center back of the skirt. Sew the waistband to the skirt with a 5/8-inch seam allowance, and stretch both pieces of fabric while you are sewing. Remember, this line of stitching must have enough stretch to be pulled over your hips.

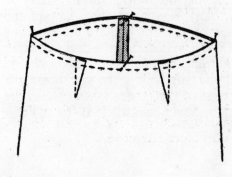

Use 1-inch-wide elastic in the waistband, and cut a strip ½ inch larger than your actual waistline measurement. Make a circle of the elastic, allowing a ½-inch overlap, and stitch securely. Quarter the elastic and pin it to the waistline seam allowance. Match the quarter marks of the elastic to the quarter marks of the waistband. Stretch the elastic to fit, and stitch it to the seam allowance only. Use a wide zig-zag stitch if you have one. If you are using a straight stitch, stretch both the elastic and the waistband while sewing. A straight stretch stitch also works well here. Keep the lower edge of the elastic slightly above the first waistline seam while you are stitching.

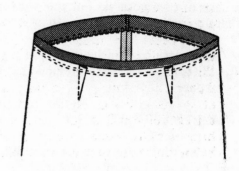

Pull the waistband over the elastic, and fold it to the back. Pin it in place, inserting the pins on the right side just below the seamline. Stitch in the seam groove from the right side. Stretch the fabric as you stitch if you are using a simple straight stitch. A zipper foot is a help for this stitching.

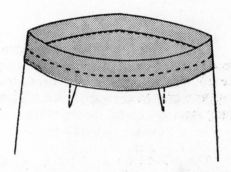

Trim the excess seam allowance from the back side of the waistband, and finish your skirt with a hem.


## THE SIMPLE KNIT SKIRT

A special knit pattern is available that can be used with knit fabrics. It does not have darts or a separate waistband, and it goes together very quickly. This kind of pattern is designed for sweater knits.

You may notice that the pattern is tapered slightly at the bottom. On sweater knits, this taper is necessary to prevent the hem from flaring as the skirt is worn. If you want to use this pattern on a doubleknit fabric, straighten the side seams to eliminate the taper. This adjustment will make your doubleknit skirt more attractive.

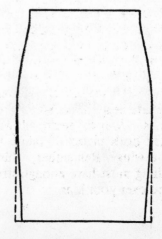

Assembling the Skirt. First sew the side seams and press them open. A string-fit is a good idea when you make this skirt for the first time because the same pattern piece is usually used for both the front and the back of the skirt. You will probably need some shaping at the waistline for a good fit. If you have to trim your skirt at the waistline, you should make note of the alteration on your pattern, so that you will make the same alteration when you make the skirt again.

Cut a piece of ¾-inch elastic that is 1 inch smaller than your waistline, and sew it to the waistline of the skirt, using the same method that is used for the pants. All that remains to be done is the hem, and you have a new skirt.

## THE MULTIPLE-GORE SKIRT

The multiple-gore skirt is a beautiful one. It can be worn with any of your knit tops, or used as a skirt for a suit. Children's skirts made in this style are also very attractive. Any doubleknit fabric can be used for the multiple-gore skirt, and you will probably want more than one in your wardrobe. Special knit patterns for this skirt are available, but it is just as easy to make your own.

The Pattern. The length of the gore will be determined by the finished length of your skirt, plus the 3½ inches needed for the hem and the turn-over waistband. The width of the gore will be 2½ inches at the top and 6½ inches at the bottom. The bottom width can be changed to 4½ inches for a child.

Determine the number of gores needed for your skirt by dividing your waistline measurement in half and adding one extra gore to that number. For example: a 26-inch waist divided in half gives 13 — add one gore for a total of 14 gores.

You will need two skirt lengths of 62-inch-wide fabric for this skirt. Remember to cut all gores with the tops directed toward the same end of the fabric so that you will not have a color change at the seamlines.

Assembling the Skirt. Press all of the gores in half lengthwise with the wrong sides together, and then stitch them together with a ¼-inch seam allowance. These seams do not have to be double-stitched, and do not press them open.

Measure 4 inches up from the skirt bottom, and clip into the stitching line on all seams. The bottom 4 inches of seam allowance should be pressed open.

CLIP→

Fold a 2-inch hem in place, and pin at the seamlines. Fold the skirt back on the seamline, right sides together. Stitch a welt along each seamline through the hem area only. Make this a narrow welt, and taper the stitching line into the original seam at the top of the hem. This stitching keeps the inside folds of the skirt sharp.

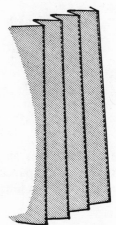

Now turn your skirt to the right side, and fold it lengthwise along the creases that you first pressed in. Stitch along these creases from the top to the bottom, making the seam as narrow as possible. Be sure to catch the back of the hem in these seamlines when you come into the hem area.

When you turn your skirt to the wrong side, you will see that the hem is caught at 2-inch intervals. This is all the hemming that is needed for this skirt. I would recommend, though, that you close the hem completely on white or pastel-colored skirts to prevent them from picking up dark lint in the hem crease when you wash the skirt, since the lint is very time-consuming to pick out.

The top of the skirt can be finished with either an elastic turned-over waistband or a separate waistband as described on page 64. Do a string fit (as described on page 47) and allow 1½ inch above the string for the turned-over finish or 5/8 inch above the string for the separate waistband finish. To reduce bulk in a turned-over finish, press the seam allowances open in the waistband area.

## THE A-LINE SKIRT

An A-line skirt can be made from a commercial pattern, or you can make your own pattern by following the instructions below. This style of skirt looks best when made from a doubleknit because it requires a fabric with body to help keep the A-line shape. The amount of flare in the skirt is up to you.

Making the Pattern. On a piece of pattern paper, draw a rectangle that is ¼ of the skirt's waistline measurement and the desired length.

Determine the waistline measurement by adding 2 inches for ease to your actual waistline measurement, and then adding an extra 2 inches for four ½-inch seams.

Example:

| | |
|---|---|
| Waist Measurement | 26" |
| Two inches for seams | 2" |
| Two inches for ease | 2" |
| | |
| Total skirt measurement | 30" |

Divide this measurement by four, and the result will be the width at the top of the pattern piece.

Determine the length of the pattern piece by adding 1½ inch for a hem, and ½ inch for a seam allowance, to the finished length of the skirt.

Example:

| | |
|---|---|
| Finished length | 20" |
| Hem | 1½" |
| Waistline seam | ½" |
| | |
| Total length | 22" |

Draw two lengthwise lines on the paper pattern, and your skirt pattern should now look the same as the illustration at the right.

Slash the pattern on the dotted lines up to, but not through, the top edge.

Place this slashed pattern piece on another folded piece of paper, and spread the strips apart until you have the desired flare. An average A-line skirt is about 45 inches around the bottom. You should have 1 to 2 inches of ease across the hipline of your skirt. Flare the pattern until you achieve this ease. Draw around the outside edge of the slashed pattern, making a new pattern piece.

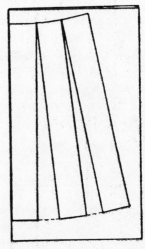

Note that the waistline and the bottom edge are now curved lines. This is correct for an A-line skirt. This pattern will require a set-on waistband. If you want to turn down elastic at the waistline, you should allow 1½ inches at the top of the pattern, instead of the ½ inch.

## A-LINE SKIRT WITH PLEATS

This is a very graceful, attractive skirt that adapts well to doubleknits. Because of the wide flare, however, this style is not recommended for striped or regularly patterned fabrics.

<u>The Pattern.</u> Use the basic A-line pattern, and divide it into thirds at the top and bottom. Do not include the seam allowance when making these divisions. Draw lines from the top to the bottom marks. These lines indicate the pleat placement.

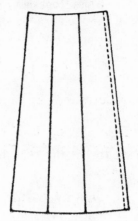

Since the skirt is flared at the bottom, the pleats must also have flare. Fold a piece of pattern paper in half, and lay it on top of the skirt pattern, with the folded edge 1 inch in from the center-front line.

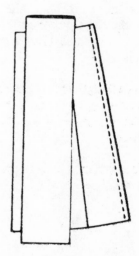

Trace the top and bottom edge of the skirt pattern onto this folded piece of pattern paper. Then trace along the line where the first pleat will be placed. Cut out this pleat pattern, and make another identical one.

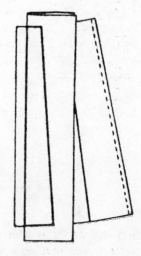

Now slash the skirt pattern along the pleat lines, and position the pleats by aligning the top and bottom of the pleat with the top and bottom of the skirt, and butting the edges together. Tape securely in place.

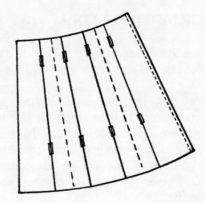

Use this pattern to cut the skirt back and skirt front. It will be placed on the fold, and two identical pieces will be cut.

You will need two skirt lengths plus 1/3 yard for this pattern. This yardage requirement is for any fabric wider than 52 inches. Remember to allow extra fabric for shrinkage.

Assembling the Skirt. Mark the top and bottom of the skirt pieces at lines A, B, C, and D. Use a small clip, a notch, or tailor's chalk.

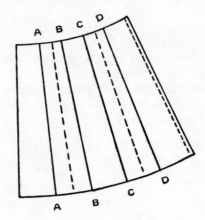

Form the pleats before you make the side seams by folding line A over to meet line B. Pin in place, and then fold line C over to meet line D. Fold and pin the other side of that skirt piece, and then use the same procedure on the other skirt piece.

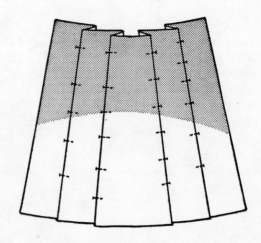

Stitch along the edge of the pleats for about 6 inches down from the waist on the right side of the skirt.

Press the pleats with a moist press cloth, and then stitch across the top of the pleats ¼ inch down from the waist edge so that they will stay in place as you apply the waistband.

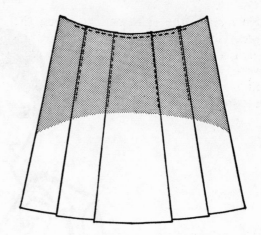

Sew the side seams, and press them open. Try on the skirt for a string fitting (refer to the PANTS section). You may need to trim at the center front and the center back to make a smooth fit in the waist area. Also check the side seams to make sure that they are perpendicular to the floor.

Cut a waistband strip across the stretch of the fabric that is 4 inches wide and 2 inches longer than your actual waistline measurement. Apply it to the skirt, using the same method that is used for the straight skirt with the separate waistband.

## V-NECKS

A V-neck finish can be used to change the style of your basic knit top or knit dress. Most of the V-necks described below can be used for men, women, and children.

One of the advantages of making a V-neck, besides the attractive style, is that you can use a strip of self fabric to trim the neck edge rather than finding a matching rib. Ribbing can be used, but self fabric is most attractive.

### THE PATTERN

A V-neck can be made from either a set-in-sleeve or a raglan-sleeve pattern. Select a pattern that already has a V-neck, or use your basic knit top pattern and cut your own V.

When you cut the garment back and front, use the low or crew-neck line. Then fold the front piece in half along the center front. Cut the V to the desired depth, starting at the center-front fold, and ending at the neck edge.

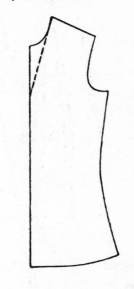

If you are using a raglan-sleeve pattern, you should first sew the sleeves to the body pieces, and then fold the garment along the center front. The cutting line for the V starts at the center-front fold and ends at the middle of the sleeve top.

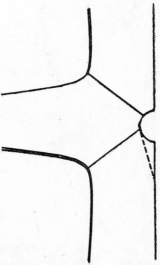

The depth of the V is up to you — but it must be large enough to pull over your head. You can cut it a little deeper than you think you would like because the trim will fill in the bottom of the V as much as 1½ to 2 inches.

By learning to cut your own V-neck, you will eliminate the need for buying many different patterns, which will not only save you money, but also space in your sewing area.

## THE TRIM

The trim for the V-neck can be of the same fabric as your garment, of a contrasting fabric, or of ribbing. Cut a 3-inch-wide strip across the greatest stretch of the fabric. You will need enough trim to go around the V-neck plus about 4 inches. Fold the trim in half lengthwise, and pin it with the wrong sides together. Do not press the trim at this point.

As you sew the trim around the V-neck, you will use slightly less trim than indicated by the neck-opening measurement. The trim will be stretched to fit as you stitch. This is very important when you are working with a very stretchy fabric or ribbing. The stretching of the trim keeps the neck edge firm. It is also important that you use the same amount of trim on each side of the V to prevent the point of the V from pulling to one side. Some measuring must be done in order to make a perfect V.

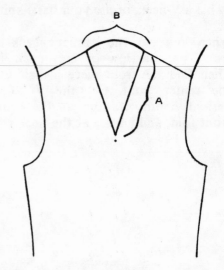

First, insert a pin from the wrong side of the garment approximately ½ inch below the point of the V. Measure the distance from this "point" pin to the shoulder seam (A). Then measure the distance from the shoulder seam to the opposite shoulder seam (B). Make sure that the fabric is flat and not stretched when you take these measurements.

Mark off 1 inch on the prepared trim, and determine how much trim is needed for the first side of the V by using the information below.

Rib trim:     for an adult, use ¾ inch less
              trim than the measured distance

              for a child, use ½ inch less trim

Self trim:    for an adult, use 3/8 inch less
              trim than the measured distance

              for a child, use ¼ inch less trim

Note: Some self trim will be very stretchy and some will be very firm. The above measurements are for firm trim. If the self trim you are using is very stretchy, use the ribbing measurements to determine how much trim is needed for each side of the V.

Subtract the amount that applies to the type of trim that you are using, and mark the result on the strip of trim with a pin.

The trim must be stretched as it is sewn around the back of the neck so that it will follow your neck curve. For every 3 inches of neck curve, you will use 2 inches of ribbing. If you are using self trim, use ½ to 1 inch less trim than the back neck measurement. The length of trim used will depend on how much stretch the trim has. Mark the amount of trim needed for the back of the neck with a pin, and then mark the amount needed for the other side of the V. Allow another inch at the end, and the trim should look like this.

## THE MITERED V-NECK

Place the right side of the trim against the right side of the V, with the cut edges even. Insert the point pin through the 1-inch mark with a ¼-inch seam allowance. Pin the next mark to the shoulder seam. Bring the trim around the back of the neck, and pin the next measured mark to the opposite shoulder seam. Now you are ready to sew.

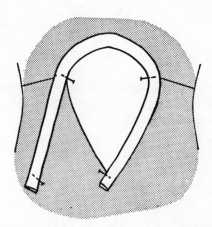

Start your stitching at the point of the V and stretch the trim to fit while you sew the side of the V. Continue stretching the trim to fit around the back of the neck, and stitch to the opposite shoulder seam.

Pin the first free end out of the way, and insert a pin from the back of the garment at the point where the stitching line started. Place the last mark over the point pin with a ¼-inch seam allowance and pin in place. Continue the stitching line from the shoulder seam to the point of the V.

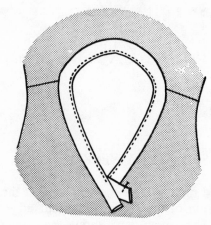

The stitching lines should meet at the point of the V for a neat finish. Be fussy, and correct the stitching, if necessary, from the wrong side.

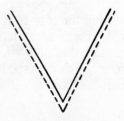

Clip the garment into the point of the V, and turn the trim to the wrong side. Fold the garment along the center front with the right sides together. Place a ruler along the fold, extending it through the trim. Draw a line along the edge of the ruler in the trim area, and stitch along this line for a perfect miter.

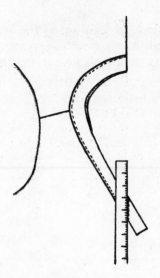

Press this seam open and the seam allowances into the garment. Then stitch the pressed-back trim at the V to the neckline seamline with either straight or zig-zag stitching. Trim the excess ends, and your V-neck is finished.

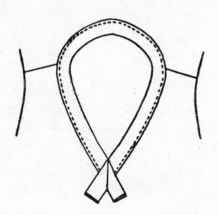
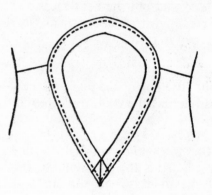

## THE CROSSED-OVER V-NECK

Pin the right side of the trim against the right side of the V, with the cut edges even. The 1-inch mark should be placed over the point pin with a ¼-inch seam allowance. Pin all but the last measured mark in their proper places. Start the stitching line 2 inches above the point of the V, stretching the trim to fit, and sew to the shoulder seam. Stretch the trim as you sew around the back of the neck, and stop your stitching at the opposite shoulder seam.

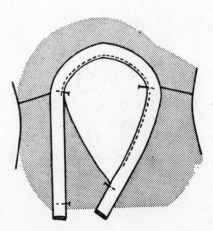

Pin the first free end out of the way, and insert a point pin from the wrong side of the garment ½ inch below the point of the V. Place the last mark over the point pin with a ¼-inch seam allowance, and then pin securely. Continue stitching from the shoulder seam to the point of the V. Clip the garment front to the point of the V, and lay it out on a flat surface, right side up.

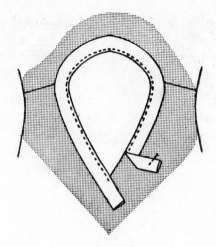

Fold over the piece of trim that was left unsewn, and tuck the free end underneath the garment.

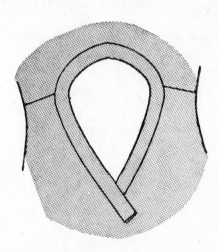

Fold over the other piece of trim, and tuck the free end through the open seam. Adjust the pieces of trim until the garment front is flat, and pin them together at the bottom of the V.

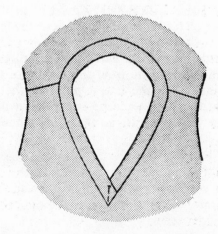

Fold over the side of the garment, and close the open seam by sewing through the garment seam allowance and the two strips of trim. The stitching line should end at the point of the V.

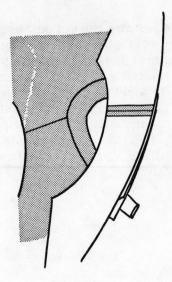

Press the neckline trim from the wrong side so that the seam allowance goes into the garment. Stitch along the seam edge with either a straight stitch or a zig-zag. Trim the excess ends for a neat finish.

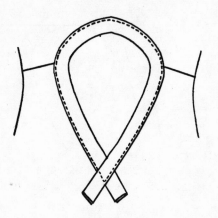 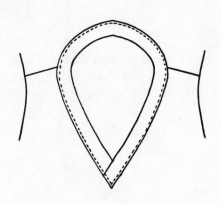

## THE V-NECK WITH AN ATTACHED DICKEY

A V-neck with a dickey must be made from a set-in sleeve pattern. Decide whether you want a crewneck or turtleneck finish, and cut the fabric using the appropriate line.

Fold the garment along the center front, and draw a line from the middle of the shoulder to the lowest point of the V. Cut the V quite deep — almost down to the waistline — for an attractive garment.

Use the V of garment fabric as a pattern for the dickey fabric. Cut the dickey ½ inch wider along the sides of the V, but the same at the neck and shoulder edges.

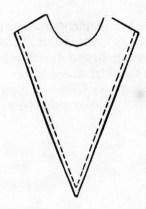

The trim for the sides of the deep V can be either self trim or ribbing, cut 3 inches wide. Insert a pin from the wrong side of the garment ½ inch below the point of the V, and measure the distance from the point pin to the shoulder edge. Determine the amount of trim needed for each side of the V from the information below. This information is for a V that ends approximately 2 inches above the waistline. Add an extra inch to the bottom of each trim strip.

Rib trim:    for an adult, use 1 inch less than the measured distance

for a child, use ¾ inch less

Self trim:    for an adult, use 5/8 inch less than the measured distance

for a child, use ½ inch less

Sew the prepared trim to each side of the V, using the mitered or crossed-over technique. Do not do the second row of stitching along the edge of the seam allowance at this point. Press the trim so that the seam allowance goes into the garment.

Pin the right side of the dickey to the wrong side of the garment front, aligning the cut edge of the dickey with the edge of the trim seam. Place the pins in the trim at about 2-inch intervals.

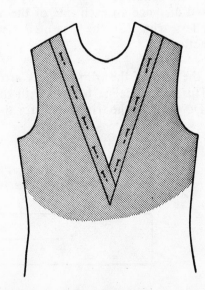

Fold over the garment front, and stitch along the trim seamline through all layers of garment and dickey fabric. Sew from the shoulder down to the point of the V, pivot the fabric on needle, and stitch up to the other shoulder edge.

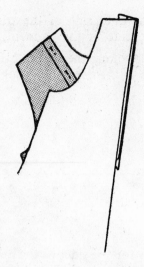

Do the second row stitching along the edge of the seam allowance. Use either a straight stitch or a zig-zag. You have just made a new garment front and are now ready to sew the shoulder seams and complete the neck trim.

### THE V-NECK WITH THE ENCLOSED MITER

Cut the garment with the desired V, and sew the left shoulder seam. Insert a pin from the wrong side of the fabric ½ inch below the point of the V. Measure the distance from the shoulder edge to the point pin (A), from the point pin the shoulder seam (B), and the distance around the back of the neck (C).

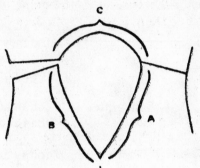

Cut a piece of trim, ribbing, or self fabric 3 inches wide. Measure the amount needed for the complete neck opening. If you are using ribbing, you will use approximately ¾ inch less trim than the measured distance on each side of the V. If you are using self fabric for the trim you will use 3/8 to ½ inch less trim than the measured distance of the V. Refer to the chart at the first part of the V-NECK section.

Mark the fold of the trim in the V-area by lightly pressing or drawing a line on the wrong side of the strip. This is a guideline to help with the miter. Mark the adjusted distances (A,B, and C) on the trim strip. Do not fold the trim in half for this application.

Place the right side of the trim against
the right side of the garment, with the
narrow edge of the trim even with the
front shoulder line. Pin the first mark to
the point pin, and stretch the trim as
you stitch a ¼-inch seam to the point
of the V.

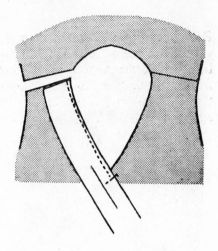

Pivot the garment and trim on the needle, and pin the next mark to the shoulder seam. Stretch
the trim to the shoulder seam as you sew, and then continue stretching it to fit as you sew around the
back of the neck.

Release the tension at the point of the V by clipping the garment front and the trim to the
stitching line. Do not cut through the stitching.

Fold the garment along the center front
with the right sides together, and pull
the fold of trim through to the wrong
side.

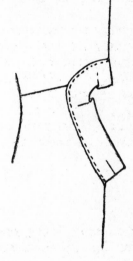

Place a ruler along the center fold, extending it through the trim. Draw a line
along the edge of the ruler up to the
middle of the trim.

Swing the ruler around and draw a line from the middle of the trim to the corner of the fold.

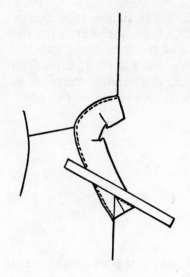

The V you have just drawn is the stitching line for the miter. Stitch along this line, clip into the point of the V, and trim, leaving a ¼-inch seam allowance. Press these two small seams open.

Stitch the garment and trim together at the shoulder line. Make sure that the trim seam allowance is pressed into the garment as you stitch across it.

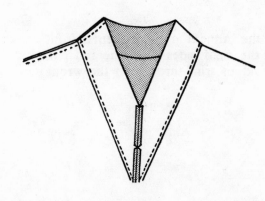

Fold the trim back on itself with the wrong sides together, and catch the free edge of the trim to the sewn edge by stitching along the original seamline or zig-zagging the trim edges together.

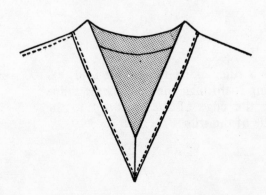

# NOTES

# THE PLACKET

There are many types of placket openings that can be used on knit garments for the whole family. The short placket with a collar is used for a man's golf shirt, as well as for adults' and children's knit tops. It can also be lengthened and used for a dress opening. The placket can be made without a collar and with trim around the neck and placket edges for another variation. A mini placket is also included in this section. It is a quick and easy neckline trim and is beautiful on knit tops and dresses.

## THE PATTERN

A basic knit-top pattern can be used for all the plackets covered in this section. You will learn how to adapt your pattern and cut the placket facing pieces. There is no need to invest in a new pattern when you can learn to make one yourself. Use the high neckline on your basic pattern for all these neckline variations.

The Collar. A collar pattern will be needed for the first placket variation. It is made from one large rectangle of fabric according to the following directions.

Measure around the seamline of the neck edge. Do not include any seam allowance in this measurement. Cut a rectangle of fabric that is the length of this measurement and 7 inches wide. This is your collar pattern, and it will be folded along the center to form the upper- and undercollar.

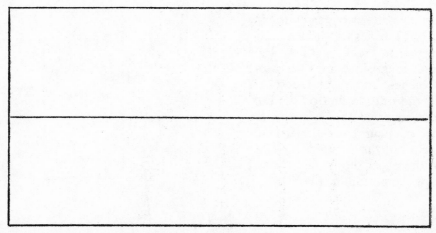

The collar can be made pointed by adding some extensions to the basic collar pattern. Measure 1 to 3 inches beyond the edge of the collar at the center-fold line. Re-draw the edges at an angle. The distance between A and B must not change because that is the part of the collar that is sewn to the neck edge. The farther out you extend the point, the more pointed your collar will become.

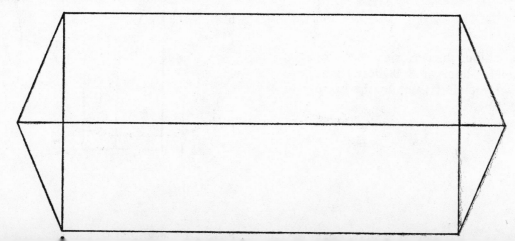

## THE PLACKET OPENING WITH A COLLAR

The technique described below can be used for sports shirts, dresses, and tops. The length of the placket is up to you. Just make the placket facings as long as you wish. Twenty-one inches is a good length for a dress placket.

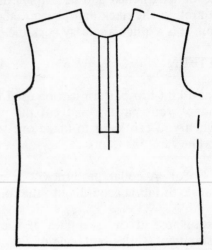

The Placket Facings. Mark the center front of the paper pattern, draw a box around the center-front line that is 1½ inches wide and as long as you want your placket opening to be.

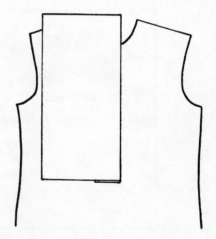

Use a piece of pattern paper or tracing paper that is 12 inches wide and about 8 inches longer than the placket box. Fold one of the long sides of the paper exactly 2 inches, and place the folded edge along the outside line of the box. Position the paper so that it covers the neck curve of your basic pattern and about 4 inches of the shoulder line. The bottom of the paper should be at least 2 inches below the bottom of the box.

Trace along the neck curve and along the shoulder line for 3 inches. Then curve down the shirt front to the bottom of the paper.

Cut along the lines that you have just drawn, and the placket facing should look like the illustration on the right.

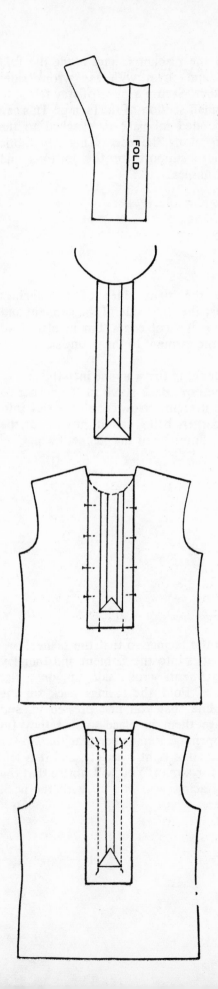

Assembling the Placket. Divide the box on the paper pattern into three ½-inch sections, and draw a wedge at the bottom that is 1 inch deep. Cut a piece of stay fabric that is 4 inches wide and 2 inches longer than the box. Trace the box design onto the stay fabric.

Mark the center-front line of the garment by pressing in a crease that is 1 inch shorter than the box. Lay the stay fabric on the wrong side of the garment front, and center the design over the center crease. Pin securely in place, making sure that the bottom of the design box is on, or parallel to, a stripe, or on the straight of the cross grain.

Use matching thread and 12 stitches to the inch to sew the outside lines of the box. Start at the center bottom of the box and stitch up to the neck edge. Again, start at the center bottom and stitch up the other side.

Cut on the inside lines of the design, but do not cut all the way into the corner of the box now.

Fold the placket facings along the fold line, and press with the wrong sides together. Secure a piece of stay fabric to the small section of the facings. This can be bonded in place or stitched to the facing along the edge. This stay fabric provides support for the buttons and buttonholes.

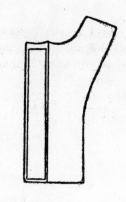

Place the right sides of the facings against the right side of the garment and line up the cut edges. Pin in place and turn the garment to the wrong side.

Stitch along the seamline into the corner of the box. Back stitch in the corner to make it secure. Now cut all the way into the corner, being careful not to cut the seam allowance of the placket facings.

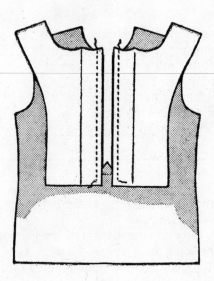

Press the facings so that the seam allowance goes into the garment and then lay the garment, wrong side up, on a flat surface. Fold the facings back on the fold line that you first pressed in, and arrange them in place so that they fill the opening. Remember that the lap for a woman is right over left, and it is left over for a man. You will notice that the neck facings will line up with the neck curve.

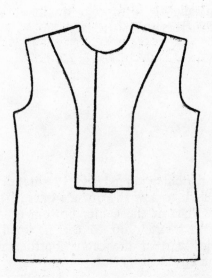

Turn the garment to the right side, and tuck the wedge into the inside of the garment. Hand-catch the lower folded edge of the top facing piece to the edge of the placket opening. This will keep things in place during the final stitching.

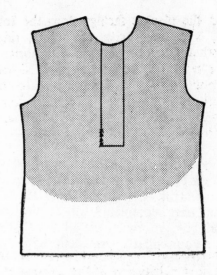

Lift the garment front until you see the wedge lying on top of the placket facings. Stitch across the base of the wedge, catching it to both facings. Press lightly from the wrong side, and remove the catch stitches. The stay fabric can now be trimmed close to the stitching lines. Sew the shoulder seams of the garment and press them.

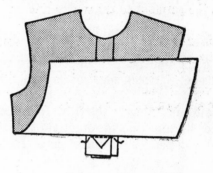

Applying the Collar. Fold the collar lengthwise with right sides together, and stitch the edges with a ¼-inch seam allowance. Turn the collar and press.

Roll under the seam allowance when pressing the collar so it will not be visible from the right side. You will find that the undercollar will have a bulge of fabric in the middle because of this rolling; carefully steam out the fullness and press so that the cut edges of the collar are even. If you choose to topstitch the collar, do so now.

Make a 1/8- to 1/4-inch cut into the undercollar at the center back. The size of the cut will be less for a lightweight knit and more for a heavy weight knit. Trim the undercollar in a dish-shaped curve, wide at the center, tapering to nothing at the corners.

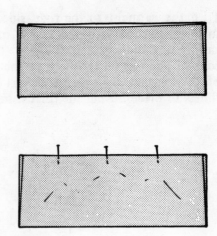

Divide the collar into four equal sections; pin the edges of the upper- and undercollar together at these marks. If you have completed all of the steps correctly, you will have a bulge that will give your collar a permanent shape and a smooth roll.

Divide the neck opening of the garment into four equal sections. Place one pin at the center back, one pin at the center front, and the other pins halfway between. Remember that the center front of the garment is in the middle of the finished placket, not on the edge of the placket.

Pin the underside of the collar to the right side of the garment, matching the quarter pins. Sew the collar to the neck edge with a ¼-inch seam allowance.

Fold the facing on the front fold line with the right side of the facing against the collar, and pin it in place. Be sure that the amount of lapel extending beyond the collar is the same on each side. Stitch the facing in place along the original seamline.

Grade the seam allowance, turn the facings to the right side, and press the back-neck seam into the shirt. Topstitch around the back of the neck to hold the seam in place.

## THE PLACKET WITH TRIM

This variation of the placket opening does not have a collar, so full facings are not needed. Instead, cut two pieces of garment fabric 4 inches wide and 2 inches longer than the finished placket. These strips will take the place of the placket facings. The neck and placket edges will be finished with ½-inch-wide trim.

Assembling the Placket. Trace the placket box onto a piece of stay fabric, just as you would do in making a regular placket opening. Press a crease along the center front of the garment, and pin the stay fabric to the wrong side of the garment front. Center the box design over the front crease, and make sure that the bottom of the box is horizontal on the fabric.

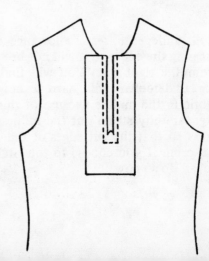

Stitch around the box using 12 stitches to the inch, and then cut along the inside lines. Do not cut all the way into the corners of the wedge at this time.

Fold the two strips of fabric in half lengthwise, with the wrong sides together, and press well. Place the strips on the right side of the garment, and align the cut edges of the strips with the cut edges of the box. Pin in place, and turn the garment to the wrong side.

Stitch along the original seamlines to the corners of the box, and backstitch to make it secure.

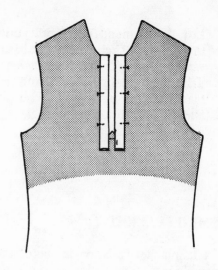

Now cut into the corners of the wedge, being careful not to cut the placket-facing seam allowance. Stitch the shoulder seams together and press.

Fold the garment along the center front and center back, and pull the two facing strips away from the garment so that they are on top of each other. Round off the top corners of the placket facings.

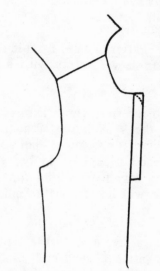

Applying the Trim. Cut a strip of trim 2½ inches wide across the stretch of the fabric. The trim can be cut from self fabric, contrasting fabric, or ribbing.

Place the right side of the trim against the right side of the placket and neck edges, and stitch it with a ½-inch seam allowance. Ease the trim around the curve at the top of the placket, and stretch it slightly around the neck curve.

Check the seam allowance to see whether it is even, and correct it if necessary. Press the trim over the seam allowance, and then fold it over to the inside of the garment. Catch it in place by stitching in the seam groove on the right side. Cut away the excess trim from the inside of the garment.

Arrange the placket pieces in place with the proper lap. Pull the wedge down to the underside, and catch the edge of the placket facing to the side of the placket opening with a few hand stitches.

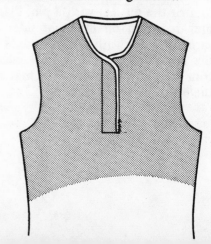

Lift the garment front until you expose the wedge. Stitch across the base of the wedge through the two facing pieces. Trim the excess stay fabric and finish the placket with buttons and buttonholes. Make the buttonholes vertical.

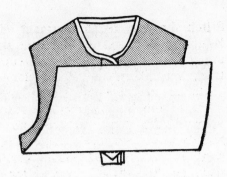

## THE MINI PLACKET

This placket variation is one of the quickest ways to finish the neckline of a knit top for a girl or woman. It is a combination of the V-neck and the placket-opening technique, and I'm sure that you will like it.

The Pattern. Use a set-in-sleeve or a raglan-sleeve pattern with a high neckline.

Fold the front garment piece in half and cut the V as illustrated at the right. Do not cut it any lower than you want the finished neck edge to be. You will be using very narrow trim for this V-neck, so it will not fill in the point of the V very much.

Press a crease along the center front of the garment the length of the finished placket.

Stitch the shoulder seams together, and press them open or to one side.

The Trim. Cut a strip of trim 1½ inches wide across the stretch of the fabric. Fold it half lengthwise with the wrong sides together, and lightly press it.

You will need enough trim to go all around the neck edge and along both sides of the crease plus about 3 extra inches.

Assembling the Placket. Mark the bottom of the placket with a pin. Place the prepared trim on the right side of the garment front with the cut edges along the center crease. Let 1 to 2 inches of trim extend below the pin that marks the bottom of the placket.

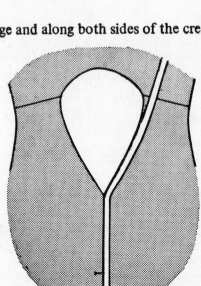

Stitch the trim to the garment with a ¼-inch seam allowance. Start the stitching line at the pin, and stitch up the trim, keeping its cut edges along the center crease. Ease the trim around the point of the V, and continue stitching around the neck. Stretch the trim slightly as you sew it to the back of the neck so that it will curve. Continue stitching along the other side of the neck until you reach the pin at the bottom of the placket. Remember to ease the trim as you stitch around the point of the V.

The beginning and the end of the stitching line should be directly opposite each other. Correct them if they are not. It is also a good idea to have both of these points secured with backstitching.

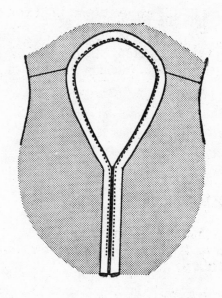

Slash down the center-front crease to within ¾ inch of the end of the stitching. Then cut to the end of the stitching lines so that a wedge is formed.

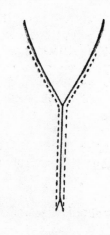

Turn the garment to the right side, and arrange the trim in its finished position. Remember that the lap is right over left for a woman. Tuck the free ends through the bottom of the placket, and pin the overlapped trim together. Baste the trim into position at the bottom of the placket so that it will not slip out of place in the final stitching.

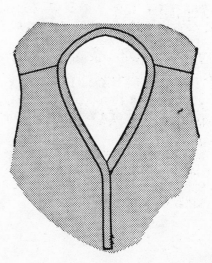

Lift the front of the garment until you see the wedge lying on top of the trim strips. Carefully stitch across the base of the wedge, catching it to the trim strips.

Do a second row of stitching around the edge of the trim seam, and press it so that the seam allowance goes into the garment. Cut away any excess trim at the bottom of the placket.

Close the placket with small buttons, which can be sewn through both layers of the placket to eliminate the need for buttonholes.

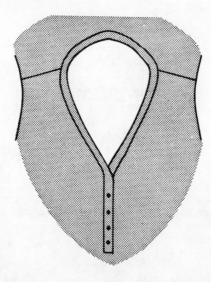

Trim that is finished 1 inch wide can be applied to a mini-placket neckline by following the above instructions with this exception: cut the trim 3 inches wide and stitch it in place with a ½-inch seam allowance instead of a ¼-inch seam allowance.

# NOTES

## MORE ZIPPERS AND TRIMS

There are many ways to trim your knit garments, and this section is designed to give you some ideas. Different neckline trims and hem variations, and two additional zipper techniques will be explained. Give some of them a try, and see how they will expand your sewing ability.

### THE EXPOSED ZIPPER THROUGH WIDE NECK TRIM

You may want to put zippers in your knit tops and dresses so that you will not have to pull the garments over your head. One zipper application has already been covered in the SHELL section. Here we will describe the technique used to place a zipper in a garment with a turtleneck or mock turtleneck.

This technique is necessary if you are using self fabric for the neckline trim because it usually does not have enough stretch to allow you to pull it over your head. The zipper can also be sewn through rib trim.

The Trim. Cut your trim strip 4 to 4½ inches wide for a mock turtleneck and 9 to 10 inches wide for a full turtleneck. The length of the trim will vary with the amount of stretch that the trim fabric has.

Generally the length should be 1 inch less than the neckline seam of the pattern. Sometimes this measurement will be too short for firm trim and too long for very stretchy trim. I suggest that you try the measured strip around your neck to see how it feels and looks before you sew it to the garment. Adjust the length if necessary. You do not have to allow a seam allowance when cutting this trim.

Press the trim in half lengthwise with the wrong sides together. This will be a guideline for zipper placement and for the finishing of the trim.

Sew the shoulder seams of the garment together, and press them open or to one side. Quarter the neck edge of the garment, and mark with pins.

Instead of sewing the trim edges together with a ¼-inch seam, you will butt the cut edges together and join them by hand or with a zig-zag stitch, thus eliminating a bulky seam at the neckline. Quarter the trim, and mark with pins.

Slip the prepared trim inside the neck edge of the garment with the right sides together. Place the trim seam at the center back, and pin the quarter marks together. Stitch the trim to the neck edge with a narrow knit seam. Press the seam into the trim. The trim should not be folded double at this point.

Applying the Zipper. Lightly press a crease along the center back of your garment. Place the zipper along this crease, with the top of the zipper teeth slightly below the fold line on the trim. Mark the bottom of the zipper teeth with a pin.

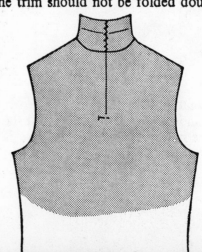

Cut a piece of stay fabric 3 inches wide and 2 inches longer than the zipper. Draw a line down the center of the stay fabric the length of the zipper. Center this line over the crease and pin the stay fabric to the right side of the garment back. The top of the line should be at the fold of the trim and the bottom of the line should be at the pin mark. Stitch along this line, using 12 stitches to the inch.

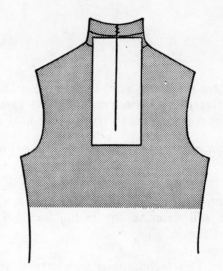

Now stitch a long box around the line that will be ¼ inch wide when completed.

Slash through the trim and cut along the center line to within ½ inch of the bottom of the box. Then cut into the corners of the box, making a wedge.

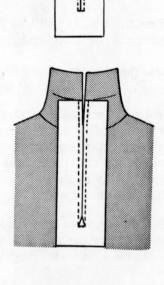

Turn all the stay fabric to the wrong side, and press it so that none of it shows on the right side. You now have a neatly faced slot.

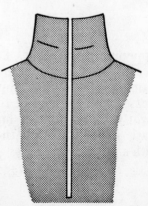

Slip the zipper into the slot, and pin it in place with the top of the zipper teeth at the fold of the trim and the metal stopper exposed at the bottom of the box. Lift the bottom of the garment until you see the wedge and the ends of the zipper tape. Stitch across the base of the wedge, securing it to the zipper tape.

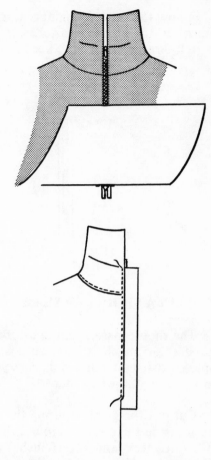

Unpin one side of the zipper and fold back the side of the garment until you see the zipper and the original stitching line. Use a zipper foot and stitch the garment to the zipper tape by sewing along this seamline. Keep the cut edge of the garment parallel to the zipper tape. You should be able to just see this through the stay fabric. Stitch from the bottom to the top. Correct your stitching from the zipper-tape side if it is not quite straight.

Unpin the other side of the zipper, fold back the other side of the garment, and stitch the zipper in from the bottom up. It is important that both stitching lines go in the same direction. Trim all the stay fabric close to seamlines.

Open the zipper and fold down the excess tape. Wrap the trim over the zipper so that the right sides of the trim are together. The bottom edge of the trim should be ¼ inch below the neck seam. Stitch through the zipper tape and both layers of trim fabric along the original seamline.

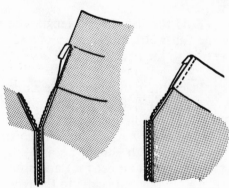

Trim the excess zipper tape and turn the neck trim right side out. You will see just the zipper teeth exposed for a neat finish.

Pin the loose neck trim in place, making sure that ¼ inch of the trim extends below the neck seamline. Finish the neck trim by stitching in the seam groove from the right side.

Another way of applying a zipper through neckline trim is to fold the trim into a double tube before you stitch it to the neck. This method is used for a basic knit top ribbing application. Use the butt seam when joining the trim rather than the regular ¼-inch seam. Quarter the neck edge, quarter the ribbing, and stitch them together with a narrow knit seam.

Follow the preceding zipper instructions, but place the top of the zipper at the top of the neck trim. After the zipper is stitched in place, you should fold the zipper tape into the garment and topstitch through the trim to keep it in place.

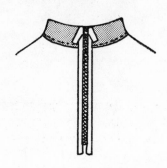
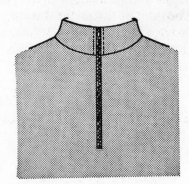

## ZIPPER IN A SHOULDER SEAM

The shoulder-seam zipper can be used with a set-in sleeve pattern. The zipper will be exposed, so a good color match is important. Since you will be stitching across the zipper teeth, buy a nylon zipper so that you will not damage your machine needle. The zipper should be long enough to extend past the edge of the shoulder.

Cut out the garment, using the high neckline on your pattern. Sew the right shoulder seam, and then measure the distance around the neck edge. Cut a strip of trim that is 4 to 4½ inches wide for a mock turtleneck, and 9 to 10 inches wide for a full turtleneck. The strip should be 1 inch less than the neck opening. However, it is always a good idea to try your measured strip of trim around your neck to see whether it is the proper size. Firm knits may need to be a bit longer and stretchy knits may need to be smaller.

Fold the trim in half lengthwise with the wrong sides together, and press the fold. Open the trim to the full width and quarter one edge of it. Quarter the neck edge, pin the marks together, and stitch the trim to the neck edge.

Place the right side of the zipper against the right side of the shoulder and trim-edge; pin in place with the top of the zipper at the fold line of the trim. The zipper teeth should be along the seam-line. Use a zipper foot and stitch on the zipper-tape side close to the teeth.

Pin the right side of the zipper to the right side of the shoulder and trim-edge on the other side of the garment, and stitch in the same manner as you did for the first side. Make sure that the neck seams are directly opposite each other on the zipper tape. The neck seam allowance should be pressed into the trim. It should be in that position when you stitch across it.

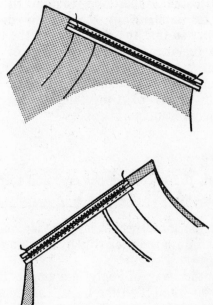

Open the zipper and fold the tape ends out of the way. Wrap the trim over the zipper so that the right sides of the trim are together. Stitch as close to the zipper teeth as you can. Trim the corner, and turn the neck trim right side out.

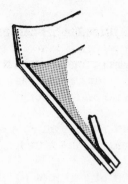

Only the zipper teeth will be exposed in the neck finish. Pin the free edge of the neckline trim over the neck seam, and stitch in the seam groove to hold it in place. Close the zipper and set the sleeve into the arm opening. Double-stitch across the zipper area, and cut away any excess zipper.

## THE ROLLED EDGE TRIM

There are many kinds of prepared trims available in fabric stores that you can use to finish the neck, arm, and front openings of knit garments. One of these is the rolled edge trim. This trim is ½ to 1½ inches wide; it is finished on both edges, but one edge has a roll to it. It is beautiful around the neck and arm openings of shells and can be used along the front of a sweater or knit jacket. The trim can be applied so that the roll goes toward either the inside or the outside of the garment. Both methods are used on ready-to-wear garments, so the choice is yours.

Place the trim along the edge of the garment with the roll going onto the right side of the fabric. There should be a 3/8-inch overlap.

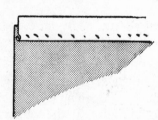

Stitch close to the beginning of the roll, catching the trim to the garment edge.

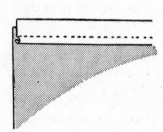

The trim is now pressed back to the inside of the garment, leaving just the roll visible from the right side. Topstitch to hold it in place, or catch it down by hand.

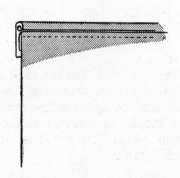

## THE RIBBED COLLAR AND CUFFS

Matching or contrasting collars and cuffs can be applied to your knit tops and dresses. The collar will stretch over your head just as a crew-neck or turtleneck does, and your hand can also slip through the cuffs so that no button opening is needed.

Use the high neckline on your basic pattern when you cut the fabric. Adjust your sleeve length so that it can accomodate the extra length that the cuffs will add.

The Collar. Cut a strip of ribbing 10 inches wide, and stretch it firmly around your head to see how much length is needed. Remember, this collar must be large enough to be pulled over your head

Place the right sides of the ribbing together and stitch down from the top edge 1 inch, and up from the bottom edge 1 inch. Backstitch at the beginning and end of these stitching lines so that they will be secure.

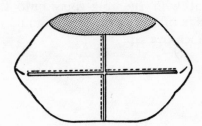

Refold the collar lengthwise so that it looks like the diagram to the right. Close the remaining opening by stitching from each folded edge to the center. Do not cross the center seam.

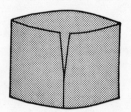

Turn the collar to the right side as illustrated.

Quarter the collar and the neck edge of the garment. Pin them right sides together with the collar seam at the center front. Stitch with a narrow knit seam.

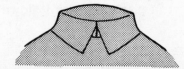

The Cuffs. The cuff is made in the same manner as the collar, but the measurements are different. The strip of cuff fabric should be about 10 inches wide and ½ inch shorter than your wrist measurement.

Instead of sewing just 1 inch down from the top and 1 inch up from the bottom, you should sew down 2½ inches, and up 2½ inches. Remember to backstitch at the beginning and end of the stitching line.

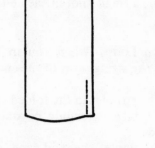

Now divide the sleeve and cuff in half and mark with pins. Slip the cuff inside the sleeve with right sides together. Position the cuff so that the wings of the cuff will be on the outside of your arm. stitch the sleeve and cuff together with a narrow knit seam.

## THE CORDED BELT OR BUTTON LOOPS

A corded belt or button loops can be made quickly from a strip of your garment fabric. These belts can dress up a plain shift or pants suit. They can also be used to make tie closures on a vest. Loop buttonholes look very elegant on your knit garments and will add a designer's touch.

Cut a strip of your knit fabric, on the lengthwise grain, as long as you need and 1 to 1½ inches wide.

You will need a piece of strong string for the narrow loops and some cotton cording for the corded belt. The string should be the length of your fabric strip, and the cording should be twice the length.

The Corded Belt. Fold the strip in half lengthwise, with the right sides together. Slip the cord down along the fold, and position it so that half the length extends beyond the end of the strip.

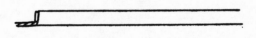

Stitch across the end of the strip, catching the cord in the stitching. Backstitch so that the cord will not slip when you begin to pull it through.

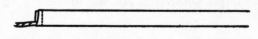

Stitch down the length of the strip, using a zipper foot. Keep the cord along the fold, and stretch the fabric while you sew. I have found that a narrow zig-zag works well here. Trim the seam allowance close to the stitching line.

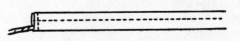

Turn the strip by pulling on the end of the cord. As you turn the strip, you will thread the cord through automatically. This saves you lots of time. Turn in the raw ends of the belt and hand-catch them closed. The belt also looks nice if you tie a small knot in each end.

Button Loops. When you are making button loops, you will not need to cord them. These are made with the string sewn to the end of the fabric strip instead of the cording.

Slip the string into the folded fabric strip with 1 inch extending beyond the end.

Stitch across the end and down the length of the strip just as you did for the corded belt. Trim the seam allowance, and pull the strip through the right side.

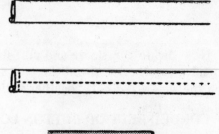

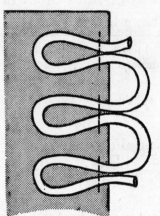

Use this long strip to form your button loops. Baste them into position before you sew the facing in place.

## THE PUFFED SLEEVE

A puffed sleeve can be made for girls' tops and dresses by stretching a strip of ribbing to fit a slightly larger sleeve than you would regularly use.

Cut the sleeve so that it is about 3 inches larger than the arm circumference when it is finished. Use the diagram at the right to help you alter the sleeve pattern. Add equally on both sides.

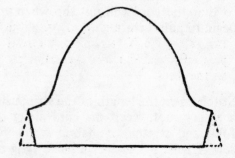

Cut a strip of ribbing that is 3 inches wide and ½ inch less than the arm circumference. Stitch the narrow ends together with a ¼-inch seam, and press the seam open with your fingers. Fold the ribbing double, and divide it into four equal sections. Divide the sleeve into four sections, and pin the ribbing to the sleeve edge with the right sides together and the marks matching.

Stretch the ribbing to fit the sleeve in each section, and stitch with a narrow seam allowance. You now have a nice puffed sleeve.

## THE CUFF HEM

This hem is very useful on the bottom and sleeves of men's sports shirts. It can also be used on pants and for hems on women's and children's tops. It is easy to do and looks almost as if a separate cuff had been sewn to the garment. You should allow a 2-inch hem for a bottom finish and a 1½-inch hem for a sleeve finish.

Fold the hem up ½ inch less than the allowed distance, with the wrong sides together. Fold the hem up again so that it looks as if you were going to make a double hem. Sew along the fold about ¼ inch from the edge, stretching slightly as you sew.

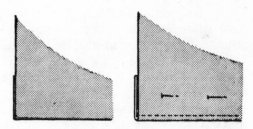

Unfold the hem and you will find that the raw edge is caught in the fold and you have a clean finish on both right and wrong sides.

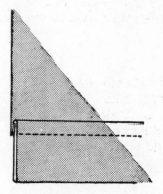

## THE MOCK EDGE TRIM HEM

This hem finish looks like trim, but is made without using a separate strip of trim. It works out nicely on tops and dresses that do not have much flare at the bottom. (Real edge trim can be applied around garments that have lots of flare.) Allow a 2-inch hem for this finish.

Fold a 2-inch hem with the right sides of the fabric together. Sew along the fold ½ inch from the edge.

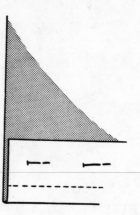

Unpin the hem, and press the free end over the seam allowance. Wrap the remaining hem around the fold to the inside of the garment. Catch the hem in place by stitching in the seam groove from the right side. Trim any excess fabric close to the stitching line on the inside.

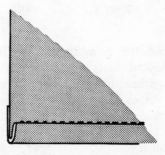

# NOTES

# BASIC PATTERN DESIGN

Designing patterns is not as difficult and complicated as you might think. You can learn a few basic design rules that will enable you to make some of your own patterns. You should start with a basic pattern that fits you well, and soon you will be able to create your own dresses and suits without having to buy a special pattern. Let your creativity go, and you will be surprised at how much fun you can have.

## DART CHANGES

The basic underarm dart can be changed to other kinds or styles of darts. One of the easiest changes is a yoke. The seam that joins the yoke to the lower part of the garment will include the fit of the dart. The basic dart can also be changed into a princess line, an armhole dart, or a French dart. These changes can give a new look to a simple, basic pattern and will enable you to create your own styles.

You must work from a basic pattern that has had the underarm dart relocated from your figure. If the basic dart is not right for you, the new pattern will not be right either. Follow these steps for simple dart changes, and work them out on pattern paper.

## THE YOKE

1.   Draw a new style line.

     The new style line for the yoke will go straight across the pattern, through the high point of the bust.

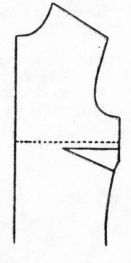

2.   Change the dressmaker's dart into a designer's dart by lengthening the end of the dart to the high point of the bust.

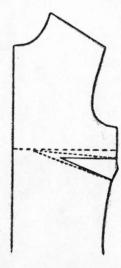

3. Remove the designer's dart by cutting along the lower leg of the dart to the high point. Overlap the cut edge of the dart to the top line of the designer's dart. Tape in place. The pattern paper should now have a bulge in it.

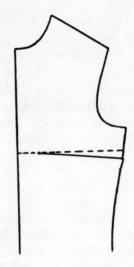

4. Cut along the new style line.

5. Add a 5/8-inch seam allowance to the cut edges.

The cutting line will be the new stitching line. When the two pattern pieces are sewn together, a bulge will again appear in the bust area.

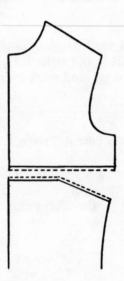

## THE PRINCESS LINE

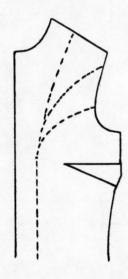

1. Draw the new style line.

   Choose the type of line you want, and draw it on your pattern. The new style line must go through the high point of the bust.

   (See left)

2. Change the dressmaker's dart to a designer's dart.

3. Remove the designer's dart.

4. Cut along the new style line.

5. Add a 5/8-inch seam allowance to the cut edges.

   (See right)

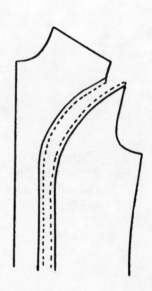

## THE PRINCESS LINE WITH A DART

1.   Draw the new style line.

     This time the style line will be 1 or
     1½ inches behind the high point of
     the bust.

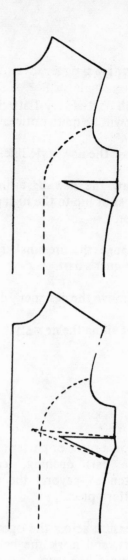

2   Change the dressmaker's dart to a
    designer's dart.

3   Remove the designer's dart.

    (See above)

4.   Cut along the new style line.

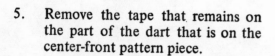

5.   Remove the tape that remains on
     the part of the dart that is on the
     center-front pattern piece.

     This dart will actually be stitched in
     the fabric before the princess line is
     sewn.

6.   Add a 5/8-inch seam allowance to
     the cut edges.

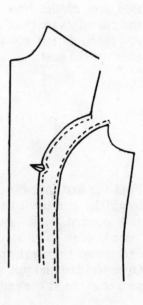

## THE FRENCH DART

A French dart is very flattering but does not produce good results in a striped fabric. The offset of the stripes will be quite noticeable on the long dart line.

1. Draw the new style line.

   Draw the new dart line from the waist or hip to the high point of the bust.

2. Change the dressmaker's dart to a designer's dart.

3. Remove the designer's dart.

4. Cut along the new style line.

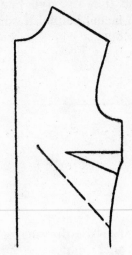

5. Tape a piece of pattern paper under the dart opening, leaving some extended beyond the edge of the pattern piece.

6. Measure across the open end of the dart, and mark the halfway point. Draw a line from that point to the high point of the bust. This is the fold line of the French dart, and the cut edges are the stitching lines. A French dart is sewn to the high point of the bust.

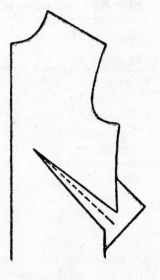

7. Fold the dart into the position that it will be in after it has been sewn and pressed. Make sure that the folded edge is down. Trim the excess paper along the pattern edge. Open the dart and you will have the proper shape at the end of the dart.

## THE ARMHOLE DART

1. Draw your new style line.

   This will extend from about the middle of the armhole to the high point of the bust.

2. Change the dressmaker's dart to a designer's dart.

3. Remove the designer's dart.

4. Cut along the new style line.

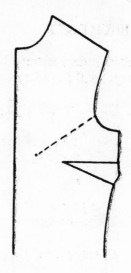

5. Tape a piece of pattern paper under the dart opening, leaving some extended beyond the edge of the pattern piece.

6. Measure across the open end of the dart and mark the halfway point. Draw a line from that point to the high point of the bust. This is the fold line of the dart, and the cut edges are the stitching lines. The armhole dart is sewn to within about 1 inch of the high point of the bust.

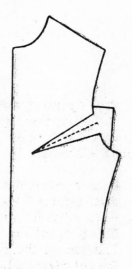

7. Fold the dart into the position that it will be in after it has been sewn and pressed. Make sure that the folded edge is down. Trim the excess paper along the pattern edge. Open the dart, and you will have the proper shape at the end of the dart.

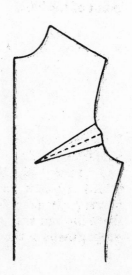

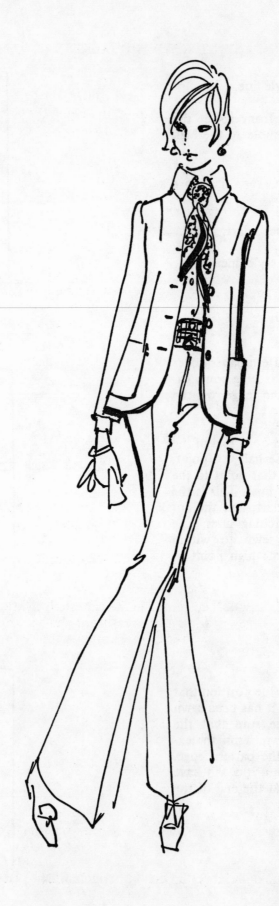

## KNIT SUITS AND JACKETS

A suit or jacket made from doubleknit fabric is very attractive, comfortable to wear, and easy to sew. Interfacing can be used in the collar and along the front edges, but linings and interlinings are not usually required. The stretch and soft look of the fabric are preserved by eliminating these items.

The pattern that you use for your knit suit or jacket can be selected from a conventional pattern catalogue or from one of the special knit series. Follow the pattern instructions to help you construct your garment and use the special techniques that are described in this section to make your project even easier

## FABRICS

Look for a firm, medium-to-heavyweight doubleknit fabric when making a suit or jacket. Polyesters and wools are recommended, and some acrylics can be used if they have enough body. Preshrink the fabric, using the method that applies to the fiber type. I suggest that you have the finished garment dry-cleaned afterward instead of washing it in order to preserve its new appearance.

## INTERFACINGS

Some lightweight interfacing is usually desirable in the collar and jacket front. I suggest using a bias cut of woven interfacing in the collar and a straight-grain cut down the front. The interfacing in the front area will support the buttons and buttonholes.

If your pattern calls for pocket flaps, I suggest that you use a lightweight interfacing there also. A press-on interfacing is nice to use in these small areas. I would not recommend using it along the front of the jacket, though.

## PATTERN ADJUSTMENTS

Check the bust dart, if your pattern has one, and change its location if necessary. Refer to the SHELL section for this information.

Look to see what kind of front facing is used in the pattern. If the front of the jacket is a straight edge, it is possible to pin the facing piece to the jacket front and eliminate the front seam. This will reduce bulk in that area. Make sure that you overlap the seamlines of the jacket front and facing when you pin them together.

## BUTTONHOLES

The buttonhole placement should also be checked to see if it is right for your figure. One buttonhole should be placed at the bustline, if possible. If you have altered the bust dart, you will probably need to change the buttonhole location. Sometimes this is not possible because of style lines or the number of buttons allowed. In that case you should have a concealed snap located at the bustline to prevent "gaposis."

Some special knit patterns do not have button and buttonhole placement marked on them, so you will have to place them yourself. The correct placement can be achieved by following these basic rules:

1.  If your jacket has an open lapel, the first buttonhole will be placed at the bustline.

2.  A double-breasted jacket will have the first buttonhole placed 1 to 2 inches below the bust.

3.    The first buttonhole placement for a jacket that buttons all the way up to the neck will be half the width of the button plus ¼ inch down from the finished neck edge of the jacket.

4.    A fitted jacket should have a button and buttonhole at the waistline.

Look at your pattern and find the center-front line. The distance between the center-front line and finished edge of the jacket will govern the size of the button that you can use. The button should be no wider than the distance between these two lines. If you choose a larger button than these lines indicate, you must increase the width between the lines so that it is at least half the width of the button plus ½ inch. This will prevent the homemade look that results when your buttons are too close to, or hanging off, the edge of the jacket.

Buttonholes always start 1/8 inch beyond the center-front line, and the buttons are sewn to the center-front line. This ensures a correct fit in a single-breasted jacket. If you are making a double-breasted jacket, the buttons and buttonholes are located an equal distance on each side of the center-front line.

The width of the buttonhole is determined by adding 1/8 inch to the width of the button. This measurement works nicely for a fairly flat button. If you have selected a round button or one that has a high dome, the width measurement is determined in a slightly different manner. Take a narrow strip of paper (about ¼ inch wide), and wrap it around the largest part of the button. The buttonhole width should be ½ that measurement.

Bound Buttonholes. Bound buttonholes are quite easy to make when using a knit fabric, and they make the garment look so much more professional. If you have had trouble with bound button-holes before, you should give this method a try, and I am sure that you will be pleasantly surprised.

The buttonholes are made before any other sewing is done on the jacket. They are worked from the right side, so all the buttonhole marks should be transferred to the right side of the garment.

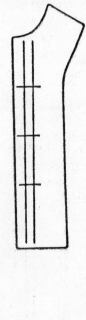

This is easy to do if you trace the buttonhole information onto your inter-facing piece. Extend the horizontal and vertical lines of the buttonholes so that the interfacing looks like the illustration at the right.

The front seam allowance of the inter-facing should be removed if you have eliminated the front seam on the jacket pattern.

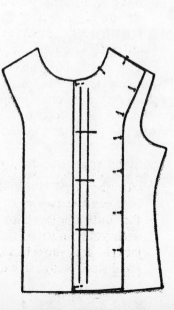

Place the interfacing on the wrong side of the right jacket front, and pin it in place securely. Stitch along the drawn lines with a contrasting thread, using the basting stitch on your machine. Stitch all horizontal lines in the same direction and all vertical lines in the same direc-tion. This is important in order to keep the lines true.

Now switch to a thread that matches the garment fabric, and set your stitch length regulator at 12 stitches to the inch.

Cut a strip of fabric 1 inch wide and long enough to give you about 6 inches for each buttonhole. Fold the strip in half with the wrong sides together, and stitch along the length of the strip approximately 1/8 inch from the fold. Now trim the folded strip so that it is twice the width of the stitched section.

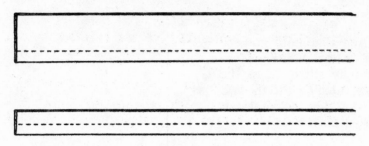

You will need two strips that are two inches longer than the buttonhole width for each buttonhole.

Working from the front of the jacket, place the cut edges of a buttonhole strip along one buttonhole line. Stitch carefully along the center of the strip between the lines that mark the buttonhole width. Make sure that you begin and end your stitching line exactly on the vertical lines and backstitch or knot your threads. This stitching line will determine the finished width of the buttonhole, so work carefully. Correct the stitching from the wrong side if necessary.

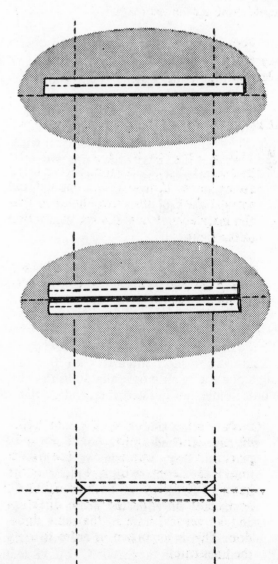

Take another buttonhole strip and butt its cut edges against the cut edges of the strip already sewn in place. Carefully stitch this one as you did the first.

Turn the jacket to the wrong side, and cut the buttonhole open by cutting between the two rows of stitching. Hold the buttonhole strips out of the way with your finger so that you cut just the jacket and interfacing fabric. Cut a good-sized wedge in each corner.

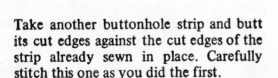

Push the strips through to the wrong side, and pull them taut. Baste the lips of the buttonhole closed.

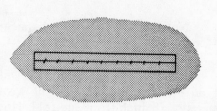

Turn the jacket to the right side, and fold back the front edge until you see the wedge lying on top of the button-hole strips. Carefully stitch across the base of the wedge, catching it to the two strips. This stitching forms the corners of the buttonhole, so make it strong.

Fold back the other side of the jacket, and expose the other wedge and strips. Stitch across the base of the wedge in the same manner as above.

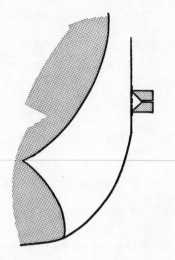

Trim the strips, leaving them about ¼ inch long. Hold your scissors at a very sharp angle when you make this cut so that it is slanted rather than blunt. This type of trimming is called grading. It will ensure that the ends of the strips will not make a ridge on the right side. Press the buttonholes from the wrong side, never from the right side.

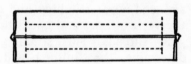

The finishing of the back of the buttonholes is left until the collar and neck edge have been completed, since the facing must be free when the collar is being applied, and the finished buttonholes would hold it down in place.

Finishing the Buttonholes. The back of a bound buttonhole is finished very easily in knit fabric. Fold the facing in place, and pin between the buttonholes. Stitch around the buttonhole from the right side with a short stitch length (20 stitches per inch) and matching thread. The needle should be going along the seam groove that joins the buttonhole strip to the jacket. Start stitching on the side of the buttonhole, not in the corner, and overlap the stitching a bit where it meets.

On the facing side of your jacket, you will have stitched a small box. Carefully open the box, and trim very closely around the stitching line. This gives a flat, neat finish to the back of the but-tonhole and the edges will not ravel.

Complete your jacket, following the instructions in the pattern. It is recommended that you use the knit hem described in the SEWING FACTS section for the jacket bottom and sleeves.

# NOTES

# THE SUIT JACKET WITH EDGE TRIM

A suit jacket with edge trim can be made from your regular jacket pattern by eliminating the collar and finishing the front, hem, and sleeve edges with edge trim. Make the jacket with a button closing, or alter the pattern for a Chanel jacket.

The trim can be of ribbing or of self fabric in a matching or contrasting color. The width of the trim can be from ¼ to 1¼ inches wide. A wider finish can be made if the trim fabric is very stretchy. Remember that the width of the finished trim is determined by the width of the seam allowance that is used when the trim is stitched in place.

When edge trim is applied to the garment, the seam allowances and hem allowances are removed in the trim area. Keep this in mind as you adjust your pattern.

## PATTERN ADJUSTMENT

Place the facing pattern in position on the front pattern, and draw a new style line. The easiest line to work with is a V. Cut both pattern pieces along this new line, and then cut away the seam allowances around the entire neck and front edges.

Cut your fabric, using these altered pattern pieces. If you are going to apply trim to the lower edges of the sleeve and jacket, you should remove or fold up the hem allowances before the fabric is cut.

A jacket that is going to button should have enough width beyond the center-front line to match the width of the finished trim. If you are using 1-inch-wide trim, there should be 1 inch of pattern between the center-front line and the pattern edge. If you are going to make the trim only ½ inch wide, the distance should be ½ inch.

A Chanel jacket, with no button closing, looks nicer if the pattern is trimmed 1 inch behind the center-front line.

## ASSEMBLING THE JACKET

Sew the shoulder seams of the jacket and facings, and press them open. Overcasting the free edge of the facing before stitching it to the jacket makes a more attractive garment.

Pin the facings in place with the wrong side of the facing against the wrong side of the jacket. Your jacket will be easier to work with if you stitch these two pieces together before you apply the trim. Straight-stitch or zig-zag along the neck and front edges.

## APPLYING THE TRIM

First, decide how wide you want the finished trim to be. Then cut the trim strips across the width of the fabric. Be sure to cut enough to finish all desired edges. If the strips are not long enough, join them together with a bias splice. The strips should be 4 times wider than the finished trim, but never smaller than 2½ inches wide.

Place the right side of the trim against the right side of the jacket and stitch, taking a seam allowance as wide as you want the finished trim to be. Stitch the trim to the jacket edge, carefully easing it around outside curves and stretching it slightly around inside curves.

Check the width of the seam allowance, and trim off any wide spots. Remember that the width of the seam allowance determines the width of the finished trim. If the seam allowance is not even, then your trim will not be even.

Press the trim over the seam allowance, and fold it to the back. The trim is finished by stitching in the seam groove on the right side of the jacket. Use a short stitch (18 per inch), with a thread matching the jacket on the top and a thread matching the trim on the bobbin. Cut the excess trim from the wrong side after the stitching is completed.

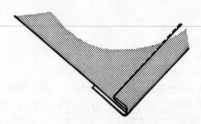

## THE MITERED CORNER

Occasionally you will design a jacket with square corners, which will require the trim to be mitered for a flat finish. Follow the instructions below for the mitered corner.

Place the trim on the right side of the garment, and stitch with the desired seam width. As you approach the corner, stop your line of stitching as far back from the corner as the seam is wide. For example: if you are using a ½-inch seam allowance, stop your stitching line ½ inch back from the corner.

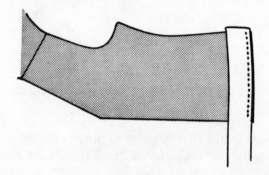

Swing the edge of the trim around the corner to the other edge of the garment. As you do this, you will notice a triangle of fabric forming at the corner. Pin the trim in place along the other edge, keeping that triangle formed, and stitch the trim to the jacket from the facing side. Stitch to the corner with the same width seam allowance, making sure that the two stitching lines meet.

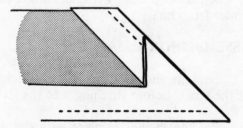

Fold the garment so that the bottom edge meets the front edge (right-angle fold). The trim should lie flat and look like the diagram at the right.

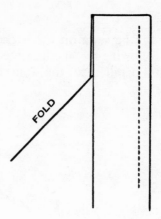

Draw a line on the trim, to the left of the seamline, the width of the seam allowance.

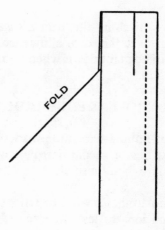

Now draw a short line on the trim from the end of the stitching to the fold of the trim.

This line is stitched and will form the miter in the corner.

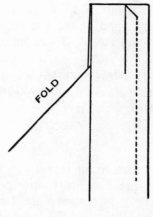

Slash the trim on the lines indicated in order to make it lie flat when turned.

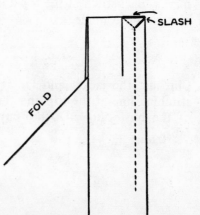

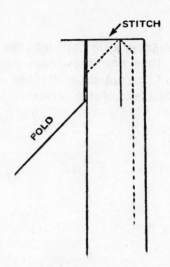

A miter can be sewn on the back of the trim by following the line indicated. This line runs parallel to the fold of the jacket fabric.

Continue stitching the trim around the rest of the garment, mitering corners where necessary. Press the trim over the seam allowance, and fold it to the back. The backs of the corners are folded into a miter and caught down when you stitch in the seam groove.

## THE BUTTONHOLE IN EDGE TRIM

This buttonhole technique works well on a jacket with either a wide or narrow trim. A small ball button works best with the narrow trim and a ¾- or 1-inch-wide button can be used on trims that are 1 inch or wider when finished.

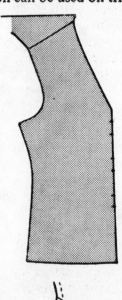

These buttonholes will be vertical, and it is a good idea to test the size needed by cutting a slit in a scrap of your fabric that is large enough to allow the button to slip through easily. Mark the buttonhole length and placement on the right front of the jacket. If you have already stitched the jacket and facing together along the edge, you should undo the stitching in the area between the buttonhole marks.

Sew the trim to the jacket edges, following the previous instructions. Do not stitch the trim between the buttonhole marks. Backstitch at the top and bottom of each buttonhole.

Clip just the jacket and facing into the stitching line at the top and the bottom of the buttonhole. Do not cut the trim fabric.

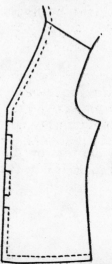

Turn these little flaps into the jacket so
that they are sandwiched between the
jacket and facing. Carefully fold back
the facing so that you expose these flaps.
Stitch along the base of the flaps to hold
them together. Trim them to ¼ inch
wide.

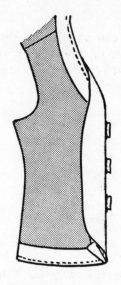

Press the trim over the seam allowance,
turn the trim to the underside, and stitch
in the seam groove. Do not stitch across
the buttonhole openings. Backstitch at
the top and bottom of the buttonholes.

Cut away the excess trim on the wrong
side of the jacket, except between the
top and bottom of the buttonholes.
Trim these flaps to the width of the
trim, and then tuck them between the
two layers of trim. Catch the folded
edges together with small hand stitches.

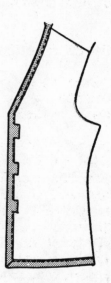

## FINISHING THE JACKET

Apply the trim to the sleeve edges and back of the jacket before you stitch the underarm seams.
Press the trim over the seam allowance, and then sew the seam with the trim in this position. Press the
seams open, and fold the trim to the back side. Catch the back of the trim by stitching in the seam
groove on the right side.

If you want the trim to go around the front of the jacket and end at the side seams, you should
cut off the hem allowance on the front of the jacket but leave it on the back of the jacket. Completely
finish the trim around the front of the jacket, and then sew the side seams together. Wrap the back
hem up around the front of the jacket, and stitch through all the layers when you make the side seam.
This makes a neat finish on the inside.

# THE ALPACA SWEATER

An alpaca sweater is a very rewarding garment to make because it looks so professional and will cost a fraction of the price of buying one. This sweater can be made for either a man or a woman, and it makes a great golf sweater because it is lightweight and can be worn year-round.

Alpaca yarn comes from an animal that lives in the mountains of South America. Because it is an animal fiber, it should be treated as wool. It is not necessary to shrink alpaca knit before cutting it, but it is recommended that you spread it on a flat surface overnight to relax the yarns.

Alpaca knit comes in tubular form with an imperfect fold along one edge. Cut the tube open along this fold so that you have a flat piece of fabric to work with.

Some alpaca knits are a blend of wool and alpaca. Check the end of the bolt so that you know what you are buying. I recommend having alpaca and alpaca blends dry-cleaned rather than washing them by hand.

## THE PATTERN

You will have to use a special knit pattern that has been designed for the alpaca golf sweater since there are no conventional patterns available for this sweater.

If you cannot find a special knit pattern, you may be able to trace a pattern from a sweater that you already have.

Place the pattern pieces on the fabric so that the grain line of the sweater knit runs up and down the sleeve and body pieces. This will necessitate placing the pattern pieces crosswise on the fabric rather than lengthwise.

The sleeve of many alpaca sweater patterns is designed very long and full so that the sleeve will bell down over the cuff. The sleeve can be made more conventional by cutting it to your exact sleeve length and tapering it at the bottom until it is about 3 inches larger than your wrist measurement. Use the same amount of ribbing as the regular sleeve width requires.

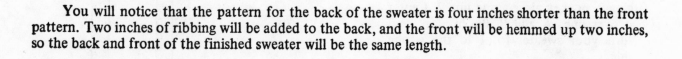

You will notice that the pattern for the back of the sweater is four inches shorter than the front pattern. Two inches of ribbing will be added to the back, and the front will be hemmed up two inches, so the back and front of the finished sweater will be the same length.

## ALPACA POCKET

If you want to add pockets to your sweater, put them in before you sew the shoulder seams.

Cut two pieces of stay fabric 4 x 7 inches. Cut two 7-x-8-inch pieces of alpaca for the pockets, making sure the grain lines are running up and down the length. Draw the following design on the stay-fabric pieces, duplicating the exact measurements.

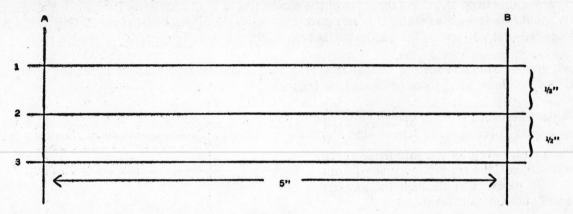

The pocket of an alpaca sweater is 5 inches long and is located on the sweater front 3 inches from the side and 5 inches up from the bottom hem. Mark the correct locations on the wrong side of the sweater front. Pin the stay-fabric piece to the wrong side of the sweater, centering line 2 of your stay design over the pocket location.

Using the long basting stitch and a contrasting thread and, sewing on the stay-fabric side, stitch the pocket design through to the right side of the sweater. Now change to a thread matching the alpaca, and do the remaining stitching at 12 stitches to the inch.

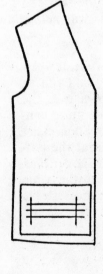

Note: When stitching parallel lines on a stay fabric, you must make sure that the stitching lines are sewn in the same direction.

Working on the right side of your sweater, place the bottom edge of your alpaca pocket piece along line 2. Center it over lines A and B. Pin in place, and turn your sweater front to the wrong side.

Stitch along line 1, starting your stitching line where line 1 crosses line A, and ending where line 1 crosses line B. Reinforce both the beginning and the end of the stitching line. Turn sweater over. Fold over the free end of the pocket 1 inch. Place the folded edge on line 3 and pin in place. Turn the sweater front to the wrong side, and stitch along line 2, reinforcing at ends where line 2 crosses lines A and B. (As above.)

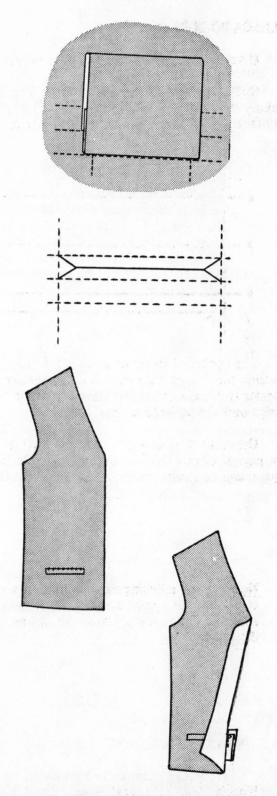

Now cut the pocket open. On the back side of the sweater, cut between lines 1 and 2, cutting a good-sized wedge at each end. Carefully cut into the corners. Do not cut the seam allowance of your pocket pieces. Cut through the sweater front and stay fabric only.

Pull the pocket piece through the cut to the wrong side. Pull the welt tight so that it fills in the pocket opening evenly. Whip the pocket closed.

Fold the sweater edge back to the pocket line, and you will see a wedge on top of your pocket pieces. Stitch across the base of the wedge through the pocket and stay fabric. The stitching line keeps the corners of the pocket closed, so do it securely. Continue stitching along the side of the pocket to close it. Do a second row of straight or zig-zag stitching.

Fold back the other edge of the sweater and stitch the base of the wedge in the same manner, continuing along the side. Trim the excess pocket edge, and press from the wrong side. Take out your whip stitches and basting threads for a finished pocket. Trim away excess stay fabric.

This pocket method can be used for your other knit fabrics also. It makes a nice pocket in a man's sports shirt. The pocket can be made wider and deeper and can be made to have a wider welt by adjusting the size of your pocket piece and stay fabric, and the measurements of the stay-fabric design.

## SHOULDER SEAMS

Sew the shoulder seams, taking a 5/8-inch seam allowance. Very little stretching is required for seams on alpaca knit. The fabric is so thick and spongy that it stretches a little just by going under the presser foot. The shoulder seam should be strengthened by another row of straight stitching in the same seamline, or by sewing a piece of seam tape into the seam. Cut the tape the same width as the shoulder on the pattern, and stitch on the tape side, rather than the sweater side. No stretching is required when using seam tape.

Trim the back seam allowance in half, and push the front seam allowance over it toward the back of the sweater. Make a welt seam by stitching on the right side ¼ inch behind the shoulder seam. This stitching can be done on the wrong side by hand, if you prefer.

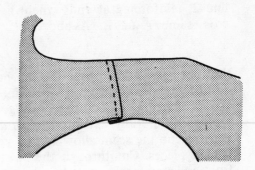

Fold the sleeve in half, and mark the center top. Pin the center-top mark to the shoulder seam, and sew the sleeve in place. The excess sleeve should be evenly distributed around the arm opening. Remember not to stretch your seams too much.

Cut a piece of alpaca ribbing 2/3 the width of the bottom of the sweater back. Fold it in half lengthwise with the right sides out. Quarter the ribbing and the sweater back, pin the quarter marks together, and then sew.

If special alpaca ribbing is not available for your sweater, you can use a piece of self fabric. Cut a strip 4½ inches wide and make sure that the grain of the alpaca goes across the strip, rather than lengthwise. Use the same 2/3 measurement for the length.

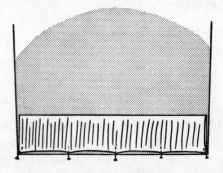

## UNDERARM SEAM AND CUFF

Sew the underarm seam by placing the right sides of the back and front together. The front will be 2 inches longer than the back. Wrap the front hem up around the back ribbing, and stitch the underarm seam. Unfold the bottom corner, and hem the sweater front by hand with a catch stitch.

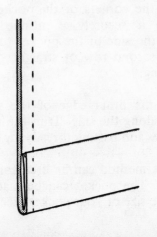

Make the cuff of the sleeve by cutting a piece of ribbing 6 inches long and stitching the cut edges with a ¼-inch seam allowance. Press the seam allowance open with your finger, and fold the ribbing back on itself so that you have a double tube of ribbing. The cuff is much smaller than the sleeve opening, but it will go in easily if you quarter the bottom of the sleeve and the cuff before you pin them together. Stretch the cuff to fit the sleeve and straight-stitch around the edge. Then do your second row of stitching, using either a straight or a zig-zag stitch. Use 6 inches of ribbing for the cuff of the men's or women's sweaters in all sizes.

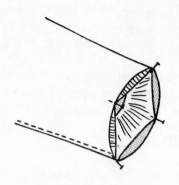

## FRONT TRIM

Use a piece of special knit trim for the front of the sweater. Steam the trim first to reduce the shrinkage, and then measure the amount needed. Take your measurements from the paper pattern, rather than from the sweater. The cut edges may have stretched out of shape a bit. Measure the distance between A and B, B and C, C and D, D and E, and E and F. Transfer these measurements to your trim.

Place the wrong side of the trim on the right side of the sweater with a 3/8-inch overlap. Pin the pre-measured marks to their proper places. There should be 2 inches of trim extending below the front edges of the sweater. Stitch 1/8 inch in from the edge of the trim, stretching slightly as you sew.

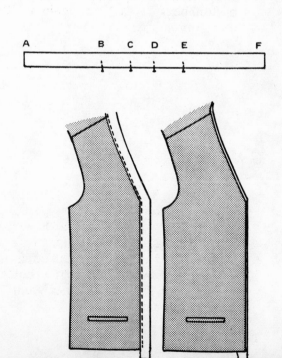

Press the trim to the wrong side of the sweater, leaving the edge of the trim visible from the right side. Turn the tag ends, and catch down by hand.

## FINISHING

The trim should be caught down around the back of the neck and 2 inches below the shoulder seam. Do this by hand, or use the blindstitch on your machine. The buttons and buttonholes will hold the trim in place along the sweater front.

Mark the buttonholes on the trim side of the sweater, and make them vertical. To keep the buttonholes trim and neat, place a piece of stay fabric between the two layers of sweater fabric before you make the buttonholes. Work the buttonholes from the trim side by machine.

## SELF TRIM

A strip of self fabric can be used to trim the edge of an alpaca sweater if the commercial trim is not available. Cut the trim on the cross grain of the fabric, and make it 3½ inches wide. Because this trim is so stretchy, it must be cut shorter than the front opening of the sweater and then stretched to fit while it is being sewn to the sweater edge.

Take the measurements for the sweater front exactly as you did when using commercial trim, but with self trim the measurements will be ¼ less for each section. The self trim will be stretched to fit and will ensure a firm neck edge as the sweater is worn.

Place the trim on the right side of the sweater with the tag end turned up. Pin the pre-measured marks in place, and stretch the trim to fit as you sew with a ½-inch seam allowance. Fold the trim to the back of the sweater, keeping the edges in the fold, and stitch in the seam groove from the right side. The raw edge of the trim can then be folded under again and caught down by hand, or it can be caught in the groove stitching. Work the buttonholes from the right side, putting a piece of stay fabric between the alpaca layers to support the buttonhole.

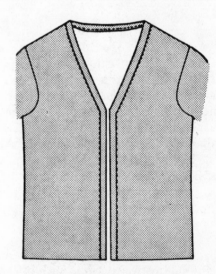

# NOTES

# SWEATERS

You can make many styles of sweaters from the sweater bodies that are available in most knit specialty shops and some regular fabric stores. Sweater bodies are tubes of sweater knit that have one edge finished with ribbing. They are made from various kinds of yarns and come in solid colors, stripes, and intricate jacquard patterns. The finished edge is used along the bottom of the sweater for a professional look, and it eliminates the need for hemming.

Some sweater bodies have another piece of ribbing attached to the bottom rib so that you will have extra for the neck or front trim. Often you can buy an extra piece of ribbing 16 to 18 inches long, that was knit especially for the neck finish.

Sweater bodies can be cut and sewn like other knit fabric without raveling. The yarns have been matted together in the knitting process and will give no problem if handled carefully.

Sweater bodies are made in different sizes, so make sure that you buy as many as you need in order to complete your garment. Many times one will be enough, but sometimes you will need two or even three to make a complete sweater.

## THE PATTERN

Sweater patterns are found only in the special knit pattern series. If these are not available to you, you can trace a pattern from a sweater that you already have.

Many cardigan sweaters are made from a pattern that does not have a side seam. This is a quick way to make a sweater, and any sweater pattern can be adapted to this technique.

Overlap the side seams of the pattern, and pin or tape them together. Place the center back of the pattern on a fold of the sweater fabric. The center front of the pattern should be ¾ inch wider than the back of the pattern to allow for the button overlap. Your pattern will look like the illustration at the right.

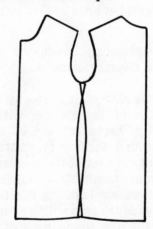

It is important that the pattern for the body and sleeves of the sweater be the exact finished length. You will be using the ribbed edge of the sweater body for the bottom of the sleeves and the sweater, which makes it difficult to adjust the length once the fabric has been cut.

## PREPARING THE FABRIC

Cut along the imperfect fold, and open the tube. Steam the sweater body to remove any bulges and to straighten the ribbed edge.

Sweater bodies can usually be cut double unless you are working with a stripe or a pattern that must be matched. You must make sure that the front opening of the sweater is cut directly along a rib on the knit. This can best be accomplished by cutting through only one layer of fabric at a time.

## SEWING SWEATER KNIT

Stitching on sweater knit will take some experimenting. You want to have a stretchy seam, but one that is flat. A rippled seam will result from too much stretching and having the stitches too close together. It is frequently necessary to lighten the pressure on the presser foot when stitching bulky sweater knits. Too much pressure will stretch the fabric as it feeds through the machine, causing rippled seams.

The seam that gives good results on one sweater knit will not necessarily produce a good seam on another type of sweater knit. Do some sample seams on scraps until you find the right combination of stitch length, stretching, and pressure.

## THE CARDIGAN SWEATER

Sew the shoulder seams of your sweater first. If there is a lot of stretch in the knit, it is a good idea to sew a piece of seam tape into the shoulder seam to stabilize it.

The method of applying the neck finish will vary with the type of trim available. Look at some of the cardigan sweaters that you own to see how the neckline trim has been finished. Determine the proper amount of trim needed by stretching the folded ribbing around your neck until it is comfortable and looks good. Allow for the ¾-inch overlap at the front of the sweater, and then cut that amount. Remember to quarter the trim and quarter the neck edge of the sweater so that you can get the neckline trim stretched evenly.

The Front Trim. The front trim is applied next and can be either 1-inch-wide grosgrain ribbon or a special knit braid that is also 1 inch wide. You will have to use what is available. If you are using grosgrain ribbon, you must shrink it before it is sewn to the sweater front. The front of the sweater will be rippled after it has been washed or cleaned if the ribbon has not been pre-shrunk

Fold the sweater along the center back, and cut two pieces of trim the length of the fold. Include the neck ribbing in this measurement.

Pin the wrong side of the trim against the right side of the sweater with a ¼-inch overlap. Leave an inch of trim extending beyond the top and bottom edge. Ease the cut edge of the sweater to fit the front trim. Many times it stretches as you are handling it. Stitch along the edge of the trim with a straight stitch. Turn the trim to the inside of the sweater and press.

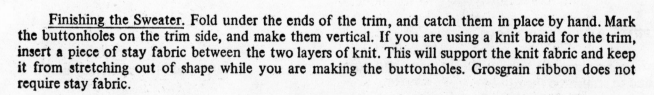

Finishing the Sweater. Fold under the ends of the trim, and catch them in place by hand. Mark the buttonholes on the trim side, and make them vertical. If you are using a knit braid for the trim, insert a piece of stay fabric between the two layers of knit. This will support the knit fabric and keep it from stretching out of shape while you are making the buttonholes. Grosgrain ribbon does not require stay fabric.

Sew the underarm seam of the sleeve, and then set the sleeve into the arm opening. Sew the buttons in place, and you have a new cardigan sweater.

A V-neck cardigan can be made for a man by using the knit braid for the front trim. Apply it in the same manner as the alpaca trim.

Old, worn sweaters can be remade into smaller sizes, using the above techniques. This is a great money-saver if you can use your husband's old sweaters and remake them for the children.

## CREW-NECK AND TURTLENECK PULLOVER SWEATERS

A crew-neck or turtleneck pullover sweater can be made from your basic knit top pattern or from one of the special knit sweater patterns. This type of neckline finish will require a piece of ribbing that matches your sweater body. It is about 4 inches wide, and must have one finished edge. This piece of ribbing can be used for a different crew-neck finish that looks very professional.

Cut the fabric, using the high neckline of the pattern. Trim the ribbing strip to 3-3/4 inches wide, and measure the amount needed by stretching it around your head. Stitch the narrow ends of the ribbing together with a ¼-inch seam allowance. Press the seam allowance open with your fingers, but do not fold the ribbing over double.

Quarter the ribbing and quarter the sweater neck. Pin the right side of the ribbing to the wrong side of the neck edge. Stretch the neck and ribbing while you sew a ½-inch seam. Use a straight stitch set at 9 stitches to the inch. Now make another seam ½ inch below the first one. The unfinished edge of the ribbing should be pinned to the neck edge in this step.

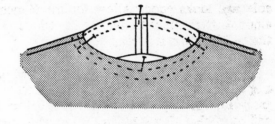

Pull the ribbing over to the right side of the sweater, and pin the finished edge of the ribbing along the bottom seamline. Catch the edge down by hand, using a backstitch. Ravel a piece of yarn from the scraps of the sweater body and use it for thread. Steam-press the yarn first in order to get rid of all its wrinkles.

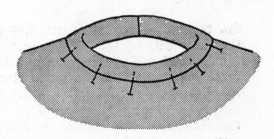

A turtleneck can be made by the same method but take just one ¼-inch seam allowance. Fold the ribbing to the right side, and catch down by hand. The ribbing could be applied in reverse by pinning the right side of the ribbing to the right side of the sweater, and then folding the ribbing to the wrong side. The hand stitching will then be on the inside of the neck edge

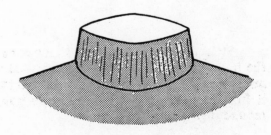

# SWIMSUITS

It is now possible to make knit swimsuits for the whole family, and they are fun to make. There are so many attractive swim fabrics available today that you will probably want more than one suit. These suits will be just as good-looking as the ones you buy but will cost half the price or even less. If you have fitting problems with ready-made suits, this is where you will solve them − so, let's get started.

## THE PATTERN

I strongly recommend that you use a special knit pattern when you make swimsuits of knit fabric. These patterns have been designed for fabrics that stretch to fit and are cut smaller than your actual measurements. Conventional patterns have been designed for fabrics with no give at all, so they are cut larger than the body measures to ensure ease of movement. These patterns would produce swimsuits that were much too large, and you probably would lose them as soon as you hit the water.

The seam allowances on knit swimsuit patterns will vary with each manufacturer, so check your pattern to see what is allowed. Women's suits are chosen according to dress size. Men's and boys' are usually sized according to the waist measurement, and little girls' suits should correspond to their clothing size.

## SWIMSUIT FABRIC

There are two types of swimsuit fabric available: those with one-way stretch, and those with two-way stretch. Fabrics with one-way stretch are used for two-piece swimsuits and men's and boys' trunks. One-way stretch fabrics have the stretch going across the width, and this stretch should go around your body. These fabrics are not suitable for one-piece swimsuits.

Two-way stretch fabrics have both crosswise and lengthwise stretch. These fabrics can be used for any type of swimsuit, and they are the only ones that will give you a comfortable fit in a one-piece suit.

Most swimsuit patterns are designed for a fabric with a 20% stretch. This means that a 15-inch strip of swimsuit fabric should be able to stretch to 18 inches. If your fabric does not stretch quite that much, you will have to use a size-larger pattern than you normally use. If the fabric stretches much more, then you can use a size-smaller pattern. Stretch your fabrics and get to know them. This will help you have well-fitting suits.

Most swimsuit fabrics are made of nylon, but you will find some made of acrylic, polyester, and combinations with spandex in them. Sometimes swimsuit fabrics will shrink, so it is a good idea to pre shrink them. If you are making a child's suit that you will be putting in the washer and dryer, pre-shrink the fabric before you cut out the pattern. Other swimsuit fabrics should be washed, but it is not necessary to put them in your dryer if you will not be drying the suit after it is made. One word of caution: some bra cups that are sewn into suits for women and girls are made of plastic. Never place these in a dryer because the heat will melt them out of shape.

Special knit fabric is available to be used for swimsuit linings. You will usually line the crotch portion of your suit and sometimes the complete suit, especially if it is white or lightweight fabric. Lining pieces are cut from your suit pattern. These are the same shape and size as the piece that they are lining.

## BRA CUPS AND ELASTIC

Bra cups are available in many different styles and sizes. There are even bra cups with padding for those who prefer this style. Some bra cups are made from plastic, but the nicest ones are made of Kodel polyester that is molded into shape. These bra cups can be machine-washed and dried. They are not affected by salt water or chlorine.

The best style of bra cup to put in a swimsuit is one that has a wide margin of lining material all around the two cups. This allows you to sew the cups into the suit for a professional look. Pin-in bra cups are also available, as well as special cups that have been designed for the woman who had undergone surgery.

The bra form for a bikini suit is usually made from a special fiberfill. You can make these yourself from a square of the padding fabric. Check the instructions in your pattern for more information on this.

You must use special elastic in your swimsuit that has been made so that it is resistant to chlorine and will hold its shape when wet. It is available in widths of 3/4, 3/8, and 1/4 inch. Check your pattern to see what width or combination of widths you will need.

## SEWING SWIMSUIT FABRIC

Swimsuit fabric is very closely knit, and you must always use a sharp, fine (#11) needle. A dull needle will have a difficult time penetrating the fabric and might cut a thread, causing the fabric to run. The new ball-point needles on the market are recommended for sewing swimsuits. Your machine should be free of lint and well oiled.

The straight stretch and overedge stretch stitches found on newer foreign-made machines are ideal for swimsuits. They produce the strong and stretchy seams that are needed in swimwear.

If you do not have one of these machines, you should make the regular knit seam as described in the SEWING FACTS section. I recommend that you use polyester thread and stretch the fabric firmly as you stitch.

Place the right sides of the front lining together. Place the right sides of the suit fronts together, and place them on top of the lining pieces. Pin together and stitch the center-front seam on the the swimsuit fabric side, making sure that you stretch firmly as you make a knit seam. Open the top layer of the suit and the bottom layer of the lining, and you will have an enclosed seam.

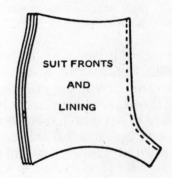

SUIT FRONTS
AND
LINING

Sew the center-back seam of the swim fabric and the center-back seam of the lining fabric separately.

The crotch seam will be sewn next. Place the right side of the suit back against the right side of the suit front and pin. Place the right side of the back lining against the right side of the front lining and pin. You will now notice that the right sides of the suit fabric are together, as are the right sides of the lining. This is the same arrangement as when you made the center-front seam and enclosed all the raw edges. Sew the crotch together with two rows of stitching, and stretch firmly as you sew. You should be stitching on the swimsuit fabric side.

While the suit is in this position, you can sew the side seams. Make sure that you place the right sides of the suit fabric together and the right sides of the lining together, and stack them on top of each other. Stretch firmly as you make a knit seam.

The trunks will now look as though you could not possibly get into them. If you will reach between the two layer of swimsuit fabric, grab the crotch section and pull it up to the right side, and you will find that it is indeed wearable and very neat, too.

## THE SEPARATE CROTCH

The separate crotch design is found on many children's and women's suits. Usually, only the crotch piece has to be lined, and that is quite a simple matter.

Place the right side of the crotch piece against the right side of the suit front. Place the right side of the crotch lining against the wrong side of the suit front. Align the cut edges, and pin in place. Sew a knit seam, taking the full width of the seam allowance but then trimming it to 1/8 inch.

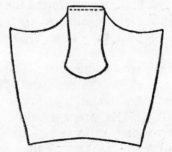

Now pin the right side of the crotch piece to the right side of the suit back. Place the suit on a flat surface with the suit back on top. Roll the suit pieces from the waist to the crotch area. You will then see the crotch lining lying on the table. Wrap this up around the rolled-up suit, and pin the right side of the crotch lining to the wrong side of the suit back. Stitch and trim the seam allowance.

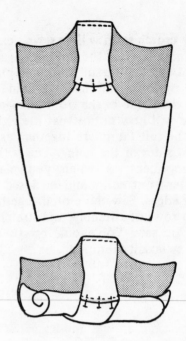

Pull the rolled-up suit out to the side of the crotch pieces, and you will have a neatly lined crotch area with no raw seams.

Occasionally you will want to line a whole suit that has a separate crotch piece. This is easily done. Assemble the whole suit first, and leave the crotch seams to last. Enclose the side seams of the suit by placing right sides of swimsuit fabric together and right sides of lining together, and placing them on top of each other. When you start lining the crotch area, you can treat the lining and swimsuit fabric of the body as one piece.

## THE BRA TOP

Assemble the bra top as your pattern instructs. You will usually have a princess line over the bust, and this will go together smoothly if you pin before you sew. The seam allowance over the high point of the bust can be kept flat and smooth if you press it toward the center of the bra, topstitch, and then trim any excess seam allowance. The bra cups will be sewn to the bra top before the bra back is joined to the bra front.

Put the bra cups on a flat surface, wrong side up, and pin the fullest part of the bra over the high point of the cups. Mold the suit over the cups, and smooth away any wrinkles in the lining fabric. Pin the bra to the bra cups all around the edges, and stitch them together along the very edge of the swimsuit fabric.

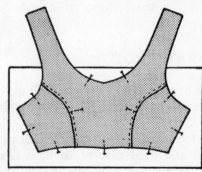

Trim any excess lining fabric, and sew the bra back to the bra front. Pin the shoulder strap seams together, and try on the bra. The straps should be snug enough to stay on as you swim. Adjust the width of the seam allowance if necessary.

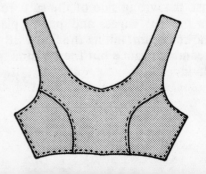

## APPLYING THE ELASTIC

Check your pattern to see what width of elastic is required around the suit edges. Two-piece suits will usually need ¾-inch elastic at the waist opening, and some will use the same width at the leg opening, while others call for 3/8-inch elastic there. You may find 3/8-inch elastic more comfortable at the leg opening, particularly if your upper thighs tend to be heavy. If your pattern calls for ¾-inch elastic but you want to use 3/8-inch elastic, you can trim the whole leg opening 3/8 inch. It is easier to do this to your pattern before you cut out your fabric rather than after the suit has been assembled.

Before you apply any elastic to the edges of your suit, it is a good idea to try the suit on so you can check the fit. A swimsuit should fit snugly because it tends to get a bit larger when it is wet. Take in or let our seams if you have to, and make a corresponding note on your pattern. Once the elastic has been applied, it is very difficult to alter the suit.

The elastic around the waist of a two-piece suit should measure the same as the waist opening. Overlap the ends ½ inch and stitch. Quarter the elastic, quarter the suit opening, pin them together and stitch, using the method described in the PANTS section.

The elastic around the leg of either one- or two-piece suits is applied in the same manner. The elastic should measure 1 inch smaller than the leg opening. When you stitch the elastic to the front of the leg, do not stretch it. But, as you stitch it to the back of the leg, stretch it 1 inch. This cups the suit around your buttocks and keeps it in place.

Place the elastic on the wrong side of the suit with the edge even with the edge of the suit. The elastic is not joined into a circle before you start to sew. It is easier if you start with the front of the leg and then stretch the elastic to fit the back.

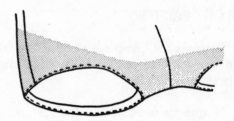

Catch the elastic to the edge of your suit with either a zig-zag or a straight stitch. If you use a straight stitch, stretch both the elastic and the suit fabric. If you use a zig-zag, you will have to stretch only the elastic to fit around the back of the leg while sewing.

Turn the elastic over itself, and stitch again on the edge of the elastic and the suit. Use either a stretch stitch or a plain straight stitch. Remember to stretch the fabric and elastic if you use the plain straight stitch.

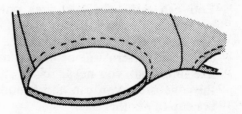

Elastic is applied around all the top edges of the one- and two-piece suits in the same manner. The elastic is the same measurement as the suit edge. That is why it is important for your suit to fit snugly before you apply the elastic. Be careful that you do not stretch the elastic in the armhole curves. This will cause your suit to cut into your arm.

The elastic will be stretched across the top of the bra about ¾ inch so that your suit will stay close to your body when you bend over. Start the stretching as soon as you finish sewing the curved area, and end it before you start sewing the curved area on the other side.

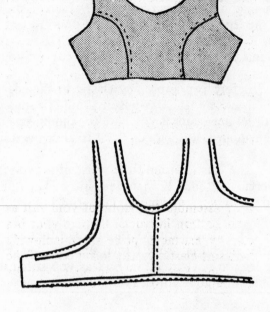

Leave ¾ inch of the bra back of a two-piece suit free of elastic. This will enable you to sew in the bra hook without having to sew through too many thicknesses of fabric.

## THE ONE-PIECE SUIT

Patterns for one-piece swimsuits usually have a brief leg or a skirt across the front, and most of them are designed with a long, flattering princess line. Remember that a one-piece suit requires a two-way stretch fabric.

If one-piece swimsuits that are ready-made do not fit you properly, there is a solution. Frequently, the size that fits your hips will be either too large or too small in the bust area. You can solve this problem by selecting a size that fits your hips, and then altering the bra portion to fit.

You can make the bust area one size larger or one size smaller by changing the size line in the bust curve only. Your complete pattern will be traced on the size lines that you need, so by altering this one area, you can accommodate a bra cup of another size.

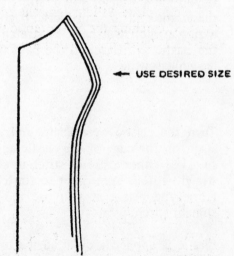

← USE DESIRED SIZE

You may have a fitting problem in length also. Your suit should be about 1 inch longer than your body measures. Take this measurement from the top of your bra to where your panties end. Compare it with your pattern accordingly. If you are long waisted, you should alter above the waistline. If you are long from the waist down, you should alter below the waist. If you are generally long in the body, you should divide the needed length equally between these two areas.

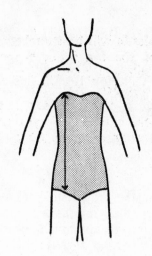

Now assemble the front of your suit as your pattern instructs. Prepare your bra cup by sewing a piece of ¾-inch-wide swimsuit elastic to the lower edge of the bra cups. Lay the elastic on top of the lining in a relaxed position, and stitch it in place. This will give more support underneath the bust and make a neat finish inside the suit.

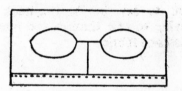

Position the bra cups underneath the suit and pin in place. Stitch along the edge of the suit, catching the lining fabric to the suit edge. Trim the excess lining fabric.

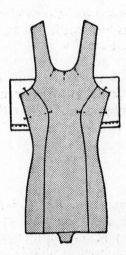

Assemble the rest of the suit, and pin the shoulder straps together. Try on the suit before you apply any elastic, and check the fit. The suit should fit tightly enough before the elastic is sewn in place so that the straps stay in place. Take a larger seam or add an extra piece of fabric if necessary. Apply the elastic to the suit edges as described previously.

## THE TANK-TOP SWIMSUIT

A tank-top swimsuit can be made from a special knit pattern, or you can make your own pattern. Make the tank top from a sleeveless-shell pattern, and make the trunks from a regular two-piece swimsuit pattern that is designed for knits. Follow the instructions below to help you adjust the sleeveless-shell pattern.

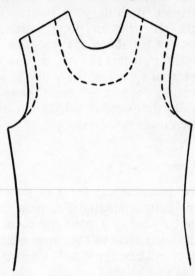

Lower the front and back of the shell pattern, and trim the arm opening larger. Lengthen the pattern if necessary. It is also important that the bust dart be in the proper location for your figure. Adjust that if necessary.

Prepare the bra cup by sewing a piece of ¾-inch swimsuit elastic to the bottom edge with enough elastic extending at the sides to be hooked at the back. Use about 3 inches less elastic than you measure around under the bust. Sew a bra hook to one end, and fold the other end over and stitch so that the hook will fit in snugly.

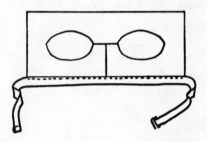

Sew the shoulder seams and darts of the tank top, and position the top over the bra cups. This is easier to do if you try on the bra cups, try on the tank top, and then adjust both to fit smoothly before pinning in place.

Stitch the bra lining to the suit around the neck opening and the sleeve opening if any is visible there. Trim any excess lining in these areas. Do not sew the bra cups into the side seam.

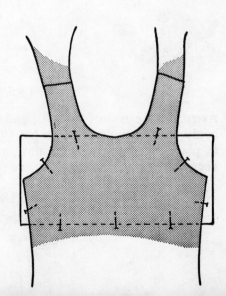

The top can now be finished by stitching 3/8-inch elastic around the neck and arm opening. Do not stretch the elastic as you sew it to the suit edge.

Elastic is not always necessary if the tank top fits well. Just turn the neck and armhole edges under ¼ inch and topstitch.

Stitch the side seams, being careful not to catch the bra lining in the seamline. Finish the top with a hem, and you have a new tank-top swimsuit.

## THE V-NECK SWIMSUIT

This technique can be used on both one- and two-piece swimsuits. The shape of the neckline must be changed into a V rather than a round neck when you make your pattern.

Cut tne center panel along the dotted line as illustrated. There is a one-inch drop from the top edge of the pattern to the bottom of the V. The dotted line has a slight curve.

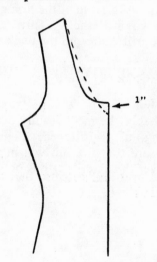

Lay a piece of ¾-inch elastic along the lower edge of the bra cups, and stitch in place.

Assemble the suit, and pin the bra cups in place. Trim the tricot in the neck area only so that it is the same shape as the suit.

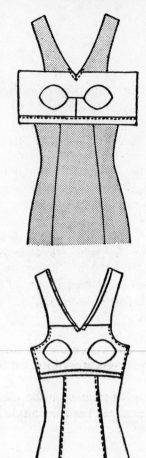

Unpin the bra cups, and place the right side of the cups against the right side of the suit. Line up the V-neck edges, and stitch the bra cups to the suit with a 3/8-inch seam allowance. Clip the suit at the point of the V to release the tension, and fold the bra cups to the wrong side of the suit. Understitch the V-neck edge, using a long stitch.

Finish the suit with elastic around the edges. When you apply elastic around the top of the suit, you will start sewing the elastic to the suit where the lining ends in the shoulder area. Stitch the elastic around the suit, and end on the opposite strap at the lining. Elastic is not sewn into the V. Turn the elastic, and topstitch around the neck edge.

## MEN'S AND BOYS' SWIM TRUNKS

Men's and boys' swim trunks can be made from one- or two-way stretch fabric. Doubleknit nylon is probably the most readily available. Some patterns have a fly front that can be made into a real fly opening, just topstitched, or ignored completely. It is a good idea to check the length of the pattern to make sure that the suit will not be too brief for the men in your family. Alter at the top or bottom, wherever the extra length is needed.

# HELPFUL HINTS

- When shrinking your fabric in the washer, use only a small amount of soap unless the fabric is dirty. Too much soap washes out the finish and makes some fabrics difficult to handle.

- Stretch terry that comes in a tube and some other bulky knit cottons will sometimes twist in the washing and drying process. You can help to preserve the straight of the grain by stitching across the open ends of the tube before shrinking it.

- When buying knits, check both sides of the fabric carefully to be sure that there are no flaws.

- Pin your stripes carefully so that they will match at the seamlines. It is easier to match stripes in a seam if you are not stretching at the same time. So do the row of zig-zag stitching first and then the straight stitching.

- A seam allowance on the turned-up portion of the hem should be trimmed in half to reduce bulk and give a smoother look on the right side.

- Children's pajamas can be made from a child's pants pattern. Taper the leg so that it measures about 4 inches larger than the ankle measurement. Cut a strip of ribbing about 6 inches wide, and sew it to the pants bottom, using the neckband technique. The ribbing should be long enough to allow the foot to slip through. The pattern can be made even simpler by overlapping the side seams of the paper pattern. This eliminates two seams and makes the pajamas quicker to sew.

- If you are going to topstitch some detail of your garment and you do not have the desired color of buttonhole twist, you can use two threads of the same color to thread the machine needle. Most of the newer machines are equipped to hold two spools of thread. If yours is not, you can wind two bobbins with your topstitching thread and stack them on top of each other on the one spindle.

- Curved seams in the underarm area of your knit garments should always be trimmed to ¼ inch, instead of clipping into the curve as you would with woven fabric. Just make sure that you stretch the seams well while you are sewing, and they will be strong enough without reinforcing.

- Occasionally you will find some patterned or striped knit fabric with a design that appears to be crooked. This distortion can occur during the finishing process when the knit fabric is given the final press. Avoid this kind of fabric because it is impossible to straighten the design, and you will have problems trying to match the fabric at seamlines.

- Self fabric can sometimes be used for a crew-neck or turtleneck finish, but it must be stretchy enough to be pulled over your head. Test the fabric by cutting a strip 3 inches wide and 14 inches long. If it will stretch to 21 inches without too much strain, then it can be used in place of ribbing.

- Make sure that all zippers and stay fabric have been pre-shrunk before you use them.

- A small wire needle threader is a handy gadget to take care of snags on your knits. Insert the small loop from the wrong side of the fabric — push the snag through the loop — then pull the wire loop back through the fabric. Do not cut off snags.

- Hair spray will dissolve any ball-point ink stains on your fabrics.

# GLOSSARY

**BALL-POINT NEEDLE**

A new sewing machine needle that is available to the home sewer. It has a rounded end that allows the needle to push between the yarns of the fabric instead of splitting them.

**BOUNCE**

The ability of a knit to return to its original shape after it has been stretched.

**BUTTONHOLE TWIST**

A heavy silk thread that is used for topstitching.

**DRESSMAKER'S DART**

The dart that you will find on your paper pattern. It is the one that is stitched.

**DESIGNER'S DART**

The dart used in basic dress design. It is drawn all the way to the point of the bust.

**EXPANDED PATTERN**

A half pattern piece that has been duplicated to create a complete front or back. It is recommended for use with striped, plaid, or evenly patterned fabrics.

**GRADING OF SEAMS**

A technique used where many layers of fabric are sewn into a single seam. All seam allowances are cut to different widths, with the widest directly under the right side of the garment.

**GROSGRAIN RIBBON**

A sturdy ribbon, used to finish the front of cardigan sweaters. It must be preshrunk.

**JACQUARD KNIT**

A fabric with an intricate design resembling that found in damask or brocade.

**KNIT SEAM**

A seam made by stretching knit fabric as it is sewn with two rows of stitching on a ¼-inch seam allowance. A straight stitch may be used on both rows, or you may use a combination of straight and zig-zag stitching.

A knit seam can also be made with the stretch stitches that are on the newer sewing machines. The fabric does not have to be stretched when these stitches are used.

**ONE-WAY STRETCH**

A characteristic of fabric that stretches in only one direction, usually across the lengthwise grain.

**OVERLAY**

An extra pattern piece that is used to modify the shape of the basic pattern piece. It is taped or pinned into position on the basic pattern. It is not cut out separately as a facing is cut.

**PATTERN PAPER**

A wide paper (45 inches) available at most knit fabric stores. Lengthwise and crosswise marks that are 1 inch apart are printed on it. It is light enough to enable you to trace patterns through it.

| | |
|---|---|
| **RAGLAN SLEEVE** | A sleeve design that does not have a conventional shoulder seam, but a diagonal seam that runs from the neck edge to the underarm. Raglan-sleeve patterns generally require more fabric than set-in sleeve patterns. |
| **RIB KNIT** | A type of fabric, used for tops and dresses, that is made of either narrow or wide ribs or a combination of the two. The most common form is a poor-boy knit. Do not confuse rib knits with ribbing. Rib knits are made with varying degrees of stretch and can sometimes be used as ribbing, but not always. |
| **ROLLED EDGE TRIM** | A commercial trim that has a permanent roll along one edge and is finished on the other. It comes in widths of 1 to 1½ inches. |
| **SELF TRIM** | A strip of fabric that is cut from the garment fabric. It is used to trim neckline and arm openings. |
| **SLEEVE CAP** | The rounded portion at the top of a sleeve pattern. It is usually too full on conventional patterns and must be altered for a smooth look. |
| **STAY FABRIC** | A lightweight, woven fabric with a firm finish that is used to give support to some details in knits. Color does not matter, but it must be pre-shrunk. |
| **STITCHING IN THE GROOVE** | A very handy technique in knit sewing. It is used to catch down facings and trims, and when applying a waistband. The needle will sew directly along the groove formed at the seamline of two pieces of fabric. |
| **TWO-WAY STRETCH** | A characteristic of fabric that stretches in both lengthwise and crosswise directions. Many swimsuit fabrics have two-way stretch. |
| **UNDERSTITCHING** | Stitching used to hold facings in place. Pull the seam allowance under the facing, and then stitch on the right side of the facing about 1/8 inch from the seamline. This catches the seam allowances to the facing and keeps the facing from rolling to the right side. |
| **WELT SEAM** | A regular seam in which both seam allowances are pressed in the same direction and then topstitched. |